Decline of Southern Steam

MICHAEL WELCH

Capital Transport

ISBN 978-1-85414-313-6

Published by
Capital Transport Publishing
P.O. Box 250, Harrow, HA3 5ZH

Printed by
1010 Printing
London SW15

Introduction

At about 5.45pm on 9th July 1967 the 2.07pm Weymouth to London train with Bulleid 'Merchant Navy' Pacific No.35030 *Elder Dempster Lines* in charge, rounded the curve into Waterloo Station. Forty minutes later, at about 6.24pm, No.35030 unceremoniously reversed out of the station and headed to Nine Elms shed, a routine that this locomotive had doubtless followed many times during its career. This was no ordinary occasion, however, because 9th July was the last day of Southern Region (SR) steam traction and the 2.07pm was the *very last* ordinary passenger working. After 130 glorious years steam traction was finally being laid to rest and everyday working steam would no longer be part of the Southern's rich heritage.

Many of the enthusiasts who witnessed those events may not have been aware that the run-down of steam traction began way back in 1909 when the South London Line was electrified. The enterprising Southern Railway further reduced the role of steam as its electrified network rapidly expanded in the 1920s/1930s. The Second World War and its aftermath put paid to such developments and it was BR's 1955 Modernisation Plan that heralded the eventual end of steam. On the SR a programme to dieselise the Hastings Line and some Hampshire local services started in 1957 and in December 1959 the first BRCW Type 3 Bo-Bo diesel locomotive arrived on the region – a major landmark in the decline of steam traction. This class eventually numbered nearly 100 machines and its introduction probably led to the withdrawal of about 300 steam locomotives. The first major post-war electrification schemes were in Kent and steam was progressively eliminated from the county between 1959 and 1961, apart from a pocket of operation around Tonbridge. The final steam-hauled 'Golden Arrow', with beautifully turned-out Bulleid 'Pacific' No.34100 *Appledore* at its head, ran from Victoria to Dover Marine and return on 11th June 1961, a forceful reminder, if one were needed, that steam really was on its way out. The year 1961 also saw the withdrawal of the delightful Adams 'Radial' tank engines from the Lyme Regis branch. During the following year the pace of withdrawals quickened as BR accountants apparently strove to reduce the number of steam locomotives inherited by the British Railways Board, which came into being on 1st January 1963. This massive purge resulted in the condemnation of the last 'Lord Nelson' and 'King Arthur' 4-6-0s plus the last represent-atives of the hugely successful 'Schools' Class. In addition, a number of 'Brighton' classes also disappeared, including the lovely Billinton K Class 'Moguls', some of which had recently been given heavy overhauls. The Beeching Report was published in the spring of 1963 and this contentious document foreshadowed the closure of many branch lines and the rationalisation of the freight business, thus rendering even more loco-motives redundant. Another significant event occurred during the summer of 1963 when the first inroads were made into the ranks of the un-rebuilt Bulleid 'Pacifics'. The next milestones in the elimination of steam occurred in 1964 when the first 'Merchant Navy' Pacifics were condemned, regular workings at Brighton ceased, steam ended on the Waterloo–Exeter route and, most importantly, government approval of the Bournemouth Electrification Scheme was announced in September. This set a date for the final withdrawal of steam traction from the region and from that time the steam fleet was apparently subjected to a delib-erate policy of neglect. Heavy overhauls ceased and maintenance was reduced to the minimum necessary in order to keep sufficient locomotives serviceable to run the advertised train service. Many locomotives were a pathetic sight, woefully neglected, covered in grime and some were shorn of name and number plates – the ultimate indignity. The final engine to be out-shopped from Eastleigh Works was No.34089 *602 Squadron* which emerged on 6th October 1966 with television cameras whirring and this melancholy occasion was widely reported in the media. Amid all of these depressing developments there were some bright spots, however, such as the generally excellent condition of Salisbury shed's fleet and the rostering of 'foreign' locomotives on various workings which often took place with the collusion of the large enthusiast fraternity employed in the operating departments! One of the most extraordinary was the appearance of 'Britannia' Pacific No. 70002 *Geoffrey Chaucer* on a Waterloo to Southampton Docks boat train on 12th May 1966. When the bitter end came there were 72 steam engines remaining on the SR's books of which many were already laid aside never to work again.

In this album, which covers the last ten years of Southern steam, I have attempted to document steam traction's inevitable decline right up to the very last day of operation. I am sure many enthusiasts keenly remember 9th July 1967, the fateful day when the glory and romance of the steam era in the south of England was suddenly consigned to history.

A special 'thank you' is due to all of the photographers who have kindly loaned their irreplaceable transparencies for publication in this volume. Without their help compilation of this book would simply not have been possible. In addition Graham Burtenshaw, Chris Evans, David Fakes, John Langford and Graham Mallinson have done an excellent job checking the manuscript and have suggested many worthwhile improvements to the text. I accept responsibility for any errors that remain.

Michael Welch

Contents

Apart from the Hastings Line, where regular steam traction on passenger trains was eliminated following the introduction of diesel units in 1957/58, the Victoria to Ramsgate/Dover route was the first main line to be modernised during the period covered by this book. Electric units replaced steam on these routes in June 1959 as part of (what was officially known as) Phase One of the Kent Coast Electrification Scheme. Up until that time services between Victoria and the Kent Coast were powered by a wonderful assortment of locomotives ranging from newly rebuilt Bulleid Pacifics to elderly South Eastern & Chatham Railway (SECR) 4-4-0s. Here a down Ramsgate train, headed by Maunsell U1 Class No.31897 of Stewarts Lane shed, makes a splendid sight as it heads out of the London suburbs at Ravensbourne on 21st July 1957. Note the immaculate condition of the uniform rake of Maunsell 1924/25 Eastern Stock carriages in carmine and cream livery. *Ken Wightman/David Clark collection*

Photographed at the same location as the previous picture, Maunsell 'Schools' Class 4-4-0 No.30915 *Brighton*, also working a down Ramsgate train, passes Ravensbourne on 9th August 1957. The train is made up of Bulleid and Maunsell vehicles in both green plus carmine and cream liveries. Following its displacement from the South Eastern Section, No.30915 spent the remainder of its BR career on the Central Section based at Redhill shed, and by mid-1962 was reported to be in extremely poor external condition. It was among the final batch of 'Schools' Class engines condemned at the end of that year and despatched to a dump of withdrawn locomotives in Hove goods yard where it joined three other 'Schools' Class locomotives Nos.30901/11/23 and a selection of other redundant motive power from the Brighton area. No.30915 was eventually scrapped at Eastleigh Works in November 1963. *Ken Wightman/David Clark collection*

During the late 1950s/early 1960s sixty of Bulleid's rather unconventional 'Light Pacifics' were rebuilt at Eastleigh Works in an effort to improve their reliability and reduce maintenance problems. The first of the rebuilt locomotives was released from Eastleigh in mid-1957 and the initial batch of locomotives to be modified included No.34001 *Exeter* which is seen here between Shortlands and Beckenham Junction with a Ramsgate to Victoria train on 4th April 1958. No.34001 was outshopped from Eastleigh in November 1957 and was obviously being kept clean by the staff at Bricklayers Arms shed, where it was based. In later years *Exeter* migrated to Nine Elms depot and subsequently Eastleigh, but it returned to the former shed and survived to the very end of steam traction on the SR, its last recorded duty being the 7.35pm Bournemouth to Waterloo train on 5th July 1967. *Ken Wightman/David Clark collection*

Opposite above: A down Kent Coast express with BR Standard Class 5MT No.73086 in charge approaches Shortlands Junction some time in the late 1950s. This locomotive was named *The Green Knight* in December 1959. In 1958 ten of these machines were based at Stewarts Lane depot and they normally seemed to be used on Ramsgate services. No.73086 later moved to the South Western Section, based at Nine Elms shed, and was withdrawn in October 1966. The line was in the course of being quadrupled at this point as part of the Kent Coast Modernisation Scheme. *Ken Wightman/David Clark collection*

Opposite below: The 'Kentish Belle' from Victoria to Ramsgate is depicted passing Shortlands on 12th July 1958 behind Bulleid Pacific No.34037 *Clovelly* which was a Ramsgate-based locomotive at the time of the photograph. This train, which was previously known as the 'Thanet Belle', was introduced in May 1948 following BR's decision to resume all-Pullman services from London to the Kent Coast. In the summer 1951 timetable the service was altered as part of the Festival of Britain celebrations and a portion for Canterbury East was detached at Faversham, returning in the evening. The remainder of the train went on to Ramsgate, serving most stations *en route*. The change of name to 'Kentish Belle' occurred in 1952 when BR decided the original name was no longer suitable and after the end of the Festival of Britain the service was changed once again to run to Ramsgate only, leaving London at 11.35am and returning from Ramsgate at 5.05pm on Mondays to Fridays. At weekends the timings were different but the train's name was still carried. Motive power during the week was normally a Bulleid Light Pacific but, at weekends, when engines were in short supply, virtually any type of main line locomotive could be observed, including SECR L Class 4-4-0s. No.34037 lasted right to the end of SR steam, gaining a place in the history books when it hauled the *very last* daylight steam departure from Waterloo, the 6.20pm boat special to Southampton Docks, on 8th July 1967. *Ken Wightman/David Clark collection*

Its burnt smokebox door and generally appalling external state indicate that the end is nigh for L Class 4-4-0 No.31766, which is seen at Canterbury East with the 7.18am Faversham to Dover Priory train on 14th June 1959, the last day of steam traction on the Victoria to Ramsgate/ Dover Priory services. The end may have been nigh for steam on this route but, amazingly, despite its decrepit condition, No.31766 survived for another eighteen months. No.31766 was based at Faversham at the time of this picture, but after electrification of the lines around that town it moved to Nine Elms shed, one of 106 Eastern Section locomotives nominally transferred to this Western Section depot hardly accustomed to maintaining SECR 4-4-0s. It is most unlikely that all of these machines actually reached their new home and some were noted dumped out of use, never to work again. No.31766 may have found employment on mundane duties such as empty stock or van trains, but is also likely to have spent lengthy periods in store before its rather charmed life was abruptly terminated by withdrawal in February 1961. Ironically, it returned to its former haunts for breaking-up, being noted on the scrap road at Ashford Works on 20th February 1961. The very last booked steam turn on the Chatham lines from Victoria was the 8.52pm to Dover Priory on the evening of 14th June, with L1 Class 4-4-0 No.31753 as motive power.
James Tawse

THE END OF STEAM ON THE CHATHAM LINE

The LSWR Adams 4-4-2Ts on the Lyme Regis branch, like the Beattie well tank engines on the Wenford Bridge line, were specially retained for working a line from which virtually all other locomotives were barred. The Axminster to Lyme Regis branch was opened in 1903 as a light railway. In order to reduce construction costs it was built with many stretches of 1 in 40 gradient and some incredibly tight curves that only short wheelbase locomotives could negotiate. In the early years of the line LBSCR 'Terriers', LSWR O2 Class 0-4-4Ts and even SECR P Class 0-6-0T locomotives were used, but all of them had shortcomings and could not match the Adams 'Radial' tank engines, their light axle load and flexible wheelbase making them ideally suited to the route. Two of these engines were used until 1946, when they were joined by a third member of the class that the Southern Railway purchased from the East Kent Railway. In this picture No.30582, a Robert Stephenson product of 1885, runs into Lyme Regis station with a train from Axminster some time during the late 1950s. *Ken Wightman/David Clark collection*

An immaculately turned-out No.30582 is seen again, this time standing in the bay platform at Axminster as the fireman apparently prepares to refill its water tank. The picture was taken on 14th May 1960, this being the last full year of operation for these graceful locomotives. Later the same year an Ivatt-designed Class 2MT 2-6-2T locomotive undertook clearance tests on the branch with the result that these machines were introduced on the line in early 1961 following track alterations. Regular steam operation ended in November 1963, but steam traction briefly reappeared in early 1965 due to a shortage of diesel units in the area. *John Langford*

FAREWELL TO THE DELIGHTFUL ADAMS 'RADIAL' LOCOMOTIVES

No.30582 is seen again this time posing at Waterloo station on 19th March 1961 prior to working a special train. It returned to its former haunts (these engines used to work LSWR suburban services) to haul a Railway Enthusiasts Club rail tour around the 'South Western' suburban lines, which included Windsor, Woking and Guildford in its itinerary. No.30582 was withdrawn in July 1961 and, regrettably, later broken-up for scrap. A representative of this much-loved class survives at the Bluebell Railway, but it is not operational at the time of writing. *Gerald Daniels*

An up continental boat train, hauled by BR Standard 'Britannia' Pacific No.70014 *Iron Duke*, approaches Bromley South on 4th August 1957. No.70014 was one of two 'Britannia' Class 7P6F locomotives (the other one was No.70004 *William Shakespeare*) allocated to Stewarts Lane shed in the early 1950s primarily for powering the prestigious 'Golden Arrow' Pullman car train between Victoria and Dover Marine and both engines were maintained in spotless external condition for this famous train. The locomotives were not confined to hauling the 'Golden Arrow', however, and sometimes put in an appearance on other boat train workings, as seen here. It was a sad day when, in May 1958, both locomotives were transferred to the London Midland Region where their superb external condition soon deteriorated. *Ken Wightman/ David Clark collection*

One of the most fascinating aspects of railways in years gone by was the profusion of cross-country through services, perhaps the most well known on the SR being the 'Pines Express' that connected Bournemouth and Manchester via the legendary Somerset and Dorset line. On the South Eastern Section there were no similar services with such a high profile but at least the multi-portioned Margate to Birkenhead train offered a worthwhile through service from many towns in Kent and Sussex to the West Midlands and Merseyside. In the summer 1957 timetable this train left Margate at 9.18am on Mondays to Fridays and ran via Canterbury West while a portion from Sandwich served Dover and Folkestone. There were also through carriages from Hastings, which ran via Eastbourne and Brighton to Redhill where they joined the main part of the train from Margate. The train travelled via Guildford, Reading and Birmingham (Snow Hill) and eventually reached Birkenhead (Woodside) at 6.37pm, so it hardly justified the description 'express service' in the timetable. At least the train conveyed a refreshment car which doubtless did a roaring trade on such a long journey. The 1957 summer Saturday timetable advertised no fewer than five separate trains from the Kent Coast to Birmingham (Snow Hill), of which the Margate service continued to Birkenhead. Some of the route traversed by these services has since been closed whilst other sections have been downgraded to secondary status. Here the Margate to Birkenhead working is depicted approaching Tonbridge behind Maunsell N Class 'Mogul' No.31403 on 12th October 1957. *Ken Wightman/David Clark collection*

A view of Charing Cross station on 1st August 1960 (a Bank Holiday Monday) showing a respectably clean D1 Class 4-4-0 No.31739 simmering at the head of a Kent Coast relief train. The photographer comments that by this date D1 Class locomotives were uncommon at Charing Cross except, perhaps, on Bank Holidays, when working empty stock or deputising for a failure. *John Langford*

A busy, everyday scene at Folkestone Junction, recorded on 20th September 1959, when steam still ruled the rails. The 12.35pm Folkestone Harbour to Victoria boat train had just arrived, having been heaved up the harbour branch by a pair of GWR pannier tank locomotives. After this massive effort the engines were recuperating at the far end of the train where a little bit of smoke is just visible. A 'Battle of Britain' Pacific, No.34073 *249 Squadron,* had quickly backed down onto the other end of the train and was 'blowing off', impatient to be on the move, and the crew seemed to be conversing with staff on the ground: perhaps they were checking that the 'panniers' had actually been uncoupled. The pair of bracket signals add more interest to the shot, as if it were needed! Note the earthworks on the right, no doubt being undertaken preparatory to electrification which occurred in the summer of 1961. Sadly, such scenes have long since disappeared and it is possible that the infamous Folkestone Harbour branch, with its incredible 1 in 30 gradient, may have been closed by the time this book is published. No.34073 ended its days at Eastleigh shed, being withdrawn in June 1964, but survives at the time of writing as a basic 'shell' and would clearly require very considerable expenditure to steam again. *John Langford*

The line between Tonbridge and Ashford is straight and fairly flat, apart from a series of minor summits, so cannot be said to be exactly bristling with points of interest for the railway aficionado. Paddock Wood station, however, used to be an exception due to its extremely fine signal box perched atop a gantry above the single track used by Hawkhurst branch trains. By the date of this photograph, 10th September 1960, the box's days were numbered and its paintwork was long overdue for attention but, even so, it was an impressive sight. The third rail is already in place on the main line tracks, but not on the Hawkhurst branch which the SR had tabled for closure. In the event passengers from Hawkhurst and intermediate stations on the branch were unable to take advantage of the new electric services introduced from 12th June 1961, because their line was shut from the same day! Here, the 4.12pm Tonbridge to Margate train is seen getting under way after its Paddock Wood station stop with Bulleid Pacific No.34016 *Bodmin* in charge and passes beneath a tall set of signals, also perched on a gantry, which controlled the junction with the Maidstone West branch. This can be seen veering off to the left beyond the signal box. The 4.12pm was a Saturdays only working that stopped at all stations and travelled via Canterbury West, reaching Margate at 6.34pm. On this particular day it was formed of BR Standard stock in colourful carmine and cream livery in contrast to the usual SR green. *John Langford*

An up boat train to London approaches Shorncliffe behind Bulleid 'Battle of Britain' Pacific No.34086 *219 Squadron* on 15th April 1961. This station has since been renamed Folkestone West. At the time of this photograph No.34086 was a Stewarts Lane engine, but was rendered redundant by the introduction of electric traction and was transferred to Exmouth Junction shed later in the year. It subsequently saw service on the Waterloo to Bournemouth line and was withdrawn in June 1966. This picture was taken just two months before the second stage of the Kent Coast Electrification Scheme became operational: note the extensive permanent way work that was being undertaken and newly installed conductor rails with their brand new insulation pots. Folkestone Central station benefited from considerable investment, a modern station with four twelve-coach platforms being constructed. This lavish provision does not appear to have been justified by the traffic levels, however, and the station has since been reduced to two tracks served by one island platform. *David Clark*

The 7.24am London Bridge to Ramsgate train was rostered for haulage by a SECR 4-4-0 until the end of steam on the London to Dover line in June 1961 and provided an opportunity to travel behind locomotives of this type that had been associated with services to the Kent Coast for so long. It would be an understatement to say that this train was popular with enthusiasts. During its final weeks of steam operation the train was heavily patronised by rail fans and others photographed it from the lineside. For a time it probably had the highest profile of any train on the South Eastern Section! In this portrait D1 Class No.31749 is depicted at Petts Wood Junction on 8th May 1961. This particular locomotive was originally built as a D Class engine at Vulcan Foundry in October 1903 and was rebuilt to a D1 Class in the 1920s. In November 1961 No.31749, accompanied by E1 Class No.31067, worked a departmental train from the London area to Ashford from where it never returned. No.31749 was cut up in January 1962 and, regrettably, no representative of either class was retained for posterity. *David Clark*

Opposite below: The down 'Golden Arrow' Pullman car train from Victoria to Dover Marine, hauled by absolutely immaculate Bulleid Pacific No.34088 *213 Squadron*, approaches Shortlands Junction. The precise date of this picture is not known, but No.34088 was rebuilt in April 1960 so the photograph must have been taken between then and electrification in June 1961. The history of Pullman trains on the London to Dover route can be traced back to 1882 when the London Chatham & Dover Railway launched a Pullman service on the route but this venture was unsuccessful. The 'Golden Arrow' first ran on 15th May 1929 and at that time motive power was usually a Maunsell 'Lord Nelson' 4-6-0, but sometimes 'King Arthur' class engines deputised. Departure time from Victoria was 11.00am. The train ceased to run in September 1939 due to the outbreak of war but resumed after the end of hostilities on 15th April 1946. In the early 1950s its departure time from London was changed to 2.00pm and it ran to Folkestone Harbour rather than Dover. In May 1960 the 'Golden Arrow' was again retimed, to leave at 11.00am, and once again ran to Dover. Steam traction was used for the last time on 11th June 1961 as a result of the inauguration of Phase Two of the Kent Coast Electrification Scheme. During the 1950s patronage started to suffer as a result of competition from the airlines and ordinary passenger coaches appeared in the formation, thus robbing the train of some of its glamour and sophistication. It was a sad day when the 'Golden Arrow' ran for the final time on 30th September 1972. *Ken Wightman/David Clark collection*

If there were ever a competition to find the 'most rebuilt station in Great Britain' Ashford would surely be a strong contender. The premises were extensively reconstructed in connection with the Kent Coast Electrification Scheme in the early 1960s, perhaps the most noticeable alteration being the conversion of two bay platforms into loops, a change that no doubt greatly improved the operational flexibility of the station. A number of mechanical signal boxes were superseded by a new panel box which was commissioned in April 1962. The station was substantially rebuilt once again in the 1990s, in rather characterless 'steel and glass' style, in connection with the introduction of Eurostar services to the continent. In this picture a somewhat travel-stained Maunsell 'Schools' 4-4-0 No.30934 *St Lawrence* pauses in the down platform with an unidentified eastbound train on 29th May 1961, just a couple of weeks prior to the start of full electric working. Built at Eastleigh Works in March 1935, No.30934 was included in the final batch of 'Schools' Class engines condemned at the end of 1962. *David Clark*

Observed from the elevated signal box at the east end of Paddock Wood station, which gave a superb panoramic view of the station and its environs, the last steam-hauled down 'Golden Arrow' hurries through on 11th June 1961 with Bulleid Pacific No.34100 *Appledore* in charge. Judging by the overcast sky, the photographer appears to have been very lucky to have the sun shining through a break in the clouds just at the right moment. There would not have been another opportunity! The bay platform on the left of the shot was used by Hawkhurst branch trains which were withdrawn from the following day. Workmen are busy (well, some of them) on the job of lengthening the down platform whilst brand new, gleaming electric units wait in the sidings before entering service the following day. *Gerald Daniels*

THE LONDON–TONBRIDGE–DOVER ROUTE RUNS OUT OF STEAM

Above: Cranbrook station on 11th September 1960, with C Class 0-6-0 No.31588 'blowing off' prior to departure with the 10.50am hop pickers' special from Paddock Wood to Hawkhurst. *John Langford*

On 28th May 1961, just a few weeks before the Hawkhurst branch was closed to all traffic, a ramblers' excursion was worked throughout from Victoria to Hawkhurst via Redhill by a pair of SECR 4-4-0s, D1 Class No.31739 and E1 Class No.31067, thus recalling the days when locomotives of this type regularly worked hop pickers' specials down the branch. *David Wigley*

A lovely picture of O1 Class No.31065 and C Class No.31592 galloping along near Goudhurst at the head of the Locomotive Club of Great Britain's (LCGB) 'South Eastern Limited' rail tour on 11th June 1961. This train's journey down the Hawkhurst branch took place during some torrential summer downpours, but the photographer seems to have chosen his spot wisely, enabling him to photograph it in brilliant sunshine. Other photographers were not so lucky and had to make do with shots taken in pouring rain: such are the frustrations of railway photography! The train was organised to mark the closure of both the Hawkhurst branch and the Kent & East Sussex (K&ESR) line which occurred that weekend. Later, participants were treated to a run along the K&ESR to Tenterden powered by a brace of 'Terriers' before returning to London behind a pair of SECR 4-4-0s. A very sad occasion but, even so, a wonderful day out which will never be repeated. *John Beckett*

Photographed during the line's last full month of operation, a Westerham branch train heading towards Dunton Green stands in Brasted station on the glorious evening of 16th September 1961. Note that the station buildings are painted in traditional SR green and cream colours and the scene is enhanced by a 'barley sugar' gas lamp standard. The train engine is SECR H Class 0-4-4T No.31308, an Ashford Works product dating from June 1906 which was equipped for 'push-pull' working in 1953 and eventually withdrawn in December 1962. The train is formed of two Maunsell carriages permanently paired for 'push-pull' operation. *David Wigley*

Photographed on a sunny autumn day, 8th October 1961, H Class 0-4-4T No.31530 propels a train to Dunton Green out of Westerham station. The branch opened on 7th July 1881 but by the date of this picture had only three weeks of life remaining. Constructed at Ashford Works in 1905, No.31530 lasted in traffic until March 1962 and was broken up at the place of its birth later the same month. *David Clark*

The Westerham branch was closed from 30th October 1961, the last trains running on 28th October. The customary motive power and coaches operated the branch until the early afternoon and here suitably decorated SECR H Class 0-4-4T No.31518 is depicted at Westerham after forming the 12.50pm service from Dunton Green. Later a seven coach set, hauled by D1 Class 4-4-0 No.31739 alternating with Q1 0-6-0 No.33029, was provided to cope with 'mourners' wishing to make a last, nostalgic trip along the line. The last train of all, the 8.30pm from Westerham, was hauled by the D1. So, the curtain came down on the penultimate Kentish branch to be regularly steam worked, parts of the redundant formation later being used for a road scheme. *John Beckett*

The Allhallows branch will go down in history as one of the shortest-lived branch lines of all time. This 1¾ miles-long line ran from Stoke Junction, on the Gravesend to Port Victoria line, to the small village of Allhallows which the over-optimistic Southern Railway hoped would develop into a large seaside resort to rival Margate and Ramsgate. The branch opened for passenger traffic on 14th May 1932 and was closed completely on 4th December 1961, becoming the fourth Kentish branch line to be closed during that year. In addition to the lines already illustrated, the remnant of the old Kent & East Sussex Railway, whose goods trains were occasionally steam worked, was closed in June 1961. The isolated position of Allhallows station is evident in this picture of SECR H Class 0-4-4T No.31518 posing there on 30th September 1961. *David Clark*

The Allhallows branch served a very sparsely populated area as exemplified here by this shot of H Class No.31308 propelling away from Middle Stoke Halt with a train to Allhallows on 29th October 1961. This small halt was one of five opened in 1906 when they were served by trains from Gravesend to Port Victoria prior to construction of the Allhallows branch. The opening of the halts resulted in the introduction of corridor coaches which enabled the guard to pass through the train to issue tickets. In an effort to stimulate traffic in the summer of 1932 the Southern Railway ran two morning trains which conveyed through carriages from Allhallows to London and corresponding evening workings, but these were soon withdrawn due to lack of patronage. *David Clark*

THE ALLHALLOWS BRANCH 1932–1961

Three veteran Beattie 0298 Class 2-4-0WTs were shedded at Wadebridge especially for working the lightly laid and tightly curved goods-only branch to Wenford Bridge and in this picture No.30585 is seen heading along the branch with empty china clay wagons on 25th April 1962. This locomotive was built as long ago as May 1874 by Beyer Peacock and, like its two sister engines, Nos.30586 and 30587, survived other members of the class by sixty years. It was not in original condition, however, having been rebuilt no less than three times during its long career. The first moves to replace the three ancient well tank locomotives were made in the spring of 1962 when GWR 0-6-0PT No.1368 arrived from Weymouth to begin trials. *John Beckett*

THE BEATTIE WELL TANKS RETIRE

By the middle of May 1962 No.1368 had reportedly passed clearance tests on Wadebridge Quay sidings and at Padstow and was due to begin trials on the Wenford Bridge branch later that month. These were obviously successful because two further members of the class later arrived from Weymouth but were temporarily put into store behind Wadebridge signal box until a water tank on the branch could be raised. The necessary arrangements were completed in August when the 0298 Class locomotives were taken out of service and sent to Eastleigh Works, where two members of the class were seen during the following month. In this shot No.1369 is depicted at Dunmere Junction with a return train from Wenford Bridge on 10th June 1964. The pannier tank locomotives lasted until about September 1964 when diesel shunters took over. No.1369 later achieved fame as the last BR steam locomotive in Cornwall and subsequently survived into preservation. *John Beckett*

The 'Lord Nelson' Class locomotives were designed by Maunsell and constructed between 1926 and 1929. They were built to haul the heaviest and fastest expresses on the Southern Railway system at that time and were considered by some people to rank among the finest and most handsome 4-6-0s ever to run in Great Britain. For a brief period in the 1920s they were the most powerful engines in the country until the GWR brought the 'Kings' into service. From 1959 onwards the entire class of sixteen locomotives was allocated to Eastleigh shed mainly for use on boat trains to and from Southampton docks. Photographs of this numerically quite small class proved to be among the most elusive of any featured in this album. Six members of the class were withdrawn in 1961 and the locomotive depicted here, No.30856 *Lord St Vincent*, was among the last four survivors: it continued in traffic until September 1962. This portrait was taken at Eastleigh shed on 16th July 1962.
Michael Chown

THE 'LORD NELSONS' BOW OUT

A fine action shot of No.30856 *Lord St Vincent* approaching Basingstoke with an up boat train from Southampton Docks on 21st July 1962. Despite being very close to withdrawal the locomotive is in quite presentable external condition. Note the rake of coaches forming the train which includes a Pullman Car in traditional umber and cream colours. The fifth vehicle in the train, which has a different body profile to other coaches, is a former Hastings gauge Pullman that has been converted for use as a buffet car, hence its green livery. The coach on the adjacent track was one of twenty vehicles built between December 1947 and July 1948 by the Birmingham Railway Carriage & Wagon Company and is of special interest because these vehicles were built with a coupé compartment (note the small sidelight) seating four passengers, rather than a normal full size compartment seating eight. *Michael Chown*

'Lord Nelson' Class No.30857 *Lord Howe* is seen in this illustration apparently shunting empty coaching stock at Basingstoke on 21st July 1962. Like all of the other members of the class No.30857 was built at Eastleigh Works and this particular locomotive entered service in December 1928. It was withdrawn in September 1962 and later cut up for scrap. *Michael Chown*

Photographed on the penultimate day of regular steam on the Chatham lines from Victoria, an unidentified 'King Arthur' Class 4-6-0 (thought to be No.30802 *Sir Durnore*) heads a Ramsgate to Victoria train over Bobbing Bank between Sittingbourne and Newington. The following day was noteworthy for the appearance of three 'King Arthur' Class locomotives in a row on evening trains from the Kent Coast to Victoria but this proved to be their swansong because the class was immediately banished from the South Eastern Section when electric traction took over the next morning. The majority of the fleet was moved to the South Western Lines but one or two members of the class were withdrawn.
John Langford

THE LAST 'KING ARTHUR' IS DEPOSED

The last of the 'King Arthur' Class engines finished their days on the South Western Lines as previously mentioned, a total of twelve surviving into 1962 based at Basingstoke, Eastleigh and Salisbury sheds. By the end of the summer, however, withdrawals had reduced this number to four, including No.30782 *Sir Brian* which was photographed on 4th August hauling the three-coach 10.10am Weymouth to Eastleigh train near Redbridge. It was withdrawn during the following month and the last example of this well-known and long-lived class, No.30770 *Sir Prianius*, was condemned in November. *Michael Chown*

The LBSCR K Class 'Moguls' were lovely locomotives – one of the author's favourite types – a very distinctive class of only seventeen examples introduced by L.B. Billinton in 1913. Five were built during that year, followed by a further batch of five during the First World War. A final batch of seven engines entered traffic in 1920/1. These powerful machines were designed for heavy freight work and spent most of their working lives on the Central Section, apart from one or two that were shedded at Fratton. They were popular engines, noted for their rugged reliability, and were also quite versatile, being pressed into service on seasonal passenger trains when the occasion demanded. Despite the fact that three examples had been given heavy overhauls in 1961, all seventeen members of the class were suddenly withdrawn towards the end of 1962 during a massive purge of steam power apparently carried out to reduce the number of steam engines inherited by the British Railways Board. The fledgling Bluebell Railway considered buying a K Class locomotive but decided they were too large for the line which used mostly small tank engines at that time. At least one locomotive remained intact until October 1964 due to the backlog in cutting-up withdrawn engines, but no saviour was forthcoming and it eventually went for scrap like all the rest. What an absolute tragedy! Here, No.32353 is seen on a special near Amberley on 24th June 1962. The 'Mogul' was in fine fettle having received a general repair only nine months previously. *John Beckett*

THE EN MASSE WITHDRAWAL OF THE LBSCR K CLASS 'MOGULS'

The seeds of destruction for steam traction on Oxted line services were sown in January 1960 when one of Eastleigh depot's 'Hampshire' DEMUs undertook trials on the route to assess the suitability of diesel electric units. The trials were satisfactory and, in late April 1962, the first 'Oxted' DEMU appeared at Tunbridge Wells West on crew training runs. Regular DEMU diagrams commenced on 18th June 1962 with two business trains in each direction on Mondays to Fridays being booked for DEMUs in place of steam. At weekends many services were formed of diesel units and the role of steam traction was much reduced, especially on services to and from London. A Tunbridge Wells West working, with BR Standard Class 4MT No.80011 in charge, leaves Oxted on 13th April 1963. The goods yard, on the left, has long since disappeared and a supermarket now adorns the site. The track of the bay platform, which goes round the back of the signal box, is still in use at the time of writing, by Uckfield line services. The use of steam traction on Oxted line trains was further reduced from 6th May 1963 when three BRCW Type 3 diesel locomotives, made redundant by freight train economies on the South Eastern Division, commenced work on the route and they were followed by many more in the ensuing weeks. On 29th June No.34013 *Okehampton* hauled the 7.17am Brighton to London Bridge train, this apparently being the last diagrammed regular Bulleid Pacific working along the line. *Michael Chown*

A London Bridge to Brighton via Eridge train, hauled by BR Standard Class 4MT 4-6-0 No.75069, takes the Edenbridge line at Hurst Green Junction in May 1963. The tracks on the left lead to East Grinstead and Hurst Green Junction signal box is visible. The author remembers that when London to Brighton via Eridge trains called at East Croydon they were always announced as terminating at Barcombe Mills to prevent unsuspecting Lewes passengers from boarding and having an extended journey. *Michael Chown*

During the spring of 1963 BR Standard Class 4MT 2-6-4Ts frequently appeared on Tunbridge Wells West to Oxted trains in place of SECR H Class 0-4-4Ts, and in this picture No.80018 approaches Hurst Green Junction with one of these workings which appears to be formed of a two-coach push-pull set. Hardly an exacting task for one of these powerful engines! No.80018 was a product of Brighton Works and it remained in service until April 1965. This picture was taken in May 1963. *Michael Chown*

Steam traction used on the Oxted to Tunbridge Wells West trains was largely unaffected by the initial mass invasion of diesel units onto other Oxted line services but diesel units took over off-peak workings on this route from the start of the 1963 summer timetable. Here, SECR H Class 0-4-4T No.31005, in quite polished external order, is pictured at Groombridge propelling one of these trains on 25th May 1963, a few weeks before most steam workings were ousted by diesels. *David Clark*

The 9.04am Oxted to Tunbridge Wells West train, with SECR H Class No.31518 in charge, leaves Hurst Green on 8th June 1963 and passes the site of the original station. Opened on 1st June 1907, Hurst Green Halt was served only by rail motor trains for many years and the facilities there consisted of wooden platforms with only rudimentary shelters. A new, much more commodious station, which could accommodate twelve-coach formations, was opened on 12th June 1961 on a different location slightly to the north of the old premises. Part of the new station's canopy and platform are just visible beyond the rear vehicle. *Michael Chown*

Opposite: The green and cream paintwork of Eridge station's buildings are a striking feature of this portrait which was taken on the sunny afternoon of 29th October 1961. It was also, apparently, an afternoon of absolutely superb cloud formations. In this shot the clouds really do seem to be in formation! Eridge was a typical country junction station which stood in splendid isolation on the Crowborough to Tunbridge Wells main road, roughly half-way between the two towns. Despite this disadvantage it offered services fanning out in four directions, to Tunbridge Wells, Brighton, Eastbourne and London via Oxted. The Beeching axe hit the area hard, however, and today Eridge is merely a wayside station on the long branch line that meanders down from Oxted to Uckfield. Trains ceased to run from there to Eastbourne in June 1965 while services to Tunbridge Wells lasted until 1985 until they, too, succumbed to closure. In this comprehensive picture the signal box plus a selection of bracket signals can be seen, and even the goods shed with its crane is visible. The train is the 12.45pm Sundays Only Eastbourne to Tunbridge Wells West hauled by BR Standard 2-6-4T No.80031 and it is awaiting the arrival of the 12.55pm Brighton to Victoria with a BR Standard Class 4MT 4-6-0 in charge. Steam traction clung on at Eridge on 'Cuckoo Line' trains until the Eastbourne line was closed, by which time steam was but a memory in most parts of Sussex. *John Langford*

The diminutive LBSCR 'Terrier' 0-6-0Ts, introduced as long ago as 1872, were primarily designed for working the East London and South London lines, and also light passenger work on short country branches. They were especially associated with the Kent & East Sussex Railway and Havant to Hayling Island branch, and some even worked on the Isle of Wight for a time. The West Quay tramway at Newhaven was another of their haunts and in this picture No.32678, built as No.78 *Knowle* in 1880, is seen carrying out some shunting work near Newhaven Town station in July 1963. The building on the right, which is still standing at the time of writing, is Newhaven shed which had been reduced to a sub-shed of Brighton by this time. The large structure in the middle of the picture was a marine engineering workshop. The sheer-legs, which are partially visible, were erected in 1877 to lift marine engines and boilers, and this 118ft-high facility was a prominent landmark in Newhaven until its demolition in August 1965. The task of working the last trains on the tramway fell to No.32678 on 10th August 1963 and this locomotive also achieved a further degree of fame when it became the last operational 'Terrier' at Brighton. *Roy Hobbs*

THE VETERAN 'TERRIERS' FINALLY LEAVE THE STAGE

After the closure of the West Quay line at Newhaven the Hayling Island branch became the last stronghold of the little 'Terriers' but even this was not destined to last for long. An extremely intensive service operated during the peak summer holiday months but business during the winter period was very slack and this, together with the allegedly poor condition of Langston viaduct, which needed repairs costing £400,000, proved to be the line's undoing. The branch was earmarked for closure in early November 1963 but during the preceding months it was very much 'business as usual'. One wonders how many of the holiday-makers who took the train to Hayling Island during the summer of that year realised they were probably making their last trip over the branch. In this portrait, No.32670 is seen approaching Langston Bridge with the 4.05pm train from Havant on 11th August 1963. This locomotive dates from 1872 and was originally LBSCR No.70 *Poplar*. It was sold to the Kent & East Sussex Railway in 1901, becoming their No.3, but returned to use on the main line system in 1948 as BR No.32670, as seen here. It should be mentioned that these engines were classified A1X by BR but were almost universally known as 'Terriers'. *Alan Chandler*

The last scheduled services along the Hayling Island branch ran on Saturday 2nd November 1963 but, on the following day when there was no public service, the LCGB ran a farewell trip using Nos.32636 and 32670. One shudders to think what the combined age of the locomotives amounted to but it must have been somewhere in the region of 180 years! Luckily, the weather for the final working was perfect and in this shot the rail tour is seen rumbling across Langston viaduct with No.32636 leading the train. It was another veteran that dated from 1872 and for many years held the distinction of being the oldest locomotive in BR stock. Note how the locomotive is completely dwarfed by the coach behind it, which appears to be the experimental glass-fibre bodied vehicle built by BR on a surplus underframe. *David Wigley*

Brighton shed was noted for keeping its engines in clean condition and in this portrait E4 Class No.32503 stands in the shed yard on 12th April 1963. This locomotive had evaded the withdrawal orders completely and continued at work on a variety of local duties throughout the spring of 1963. Sadly, the day after this picture was taken it set off on its last journey to Eastleigh but at least it had a footnote in history as the penultimate representative of its class at Brighton, because No.32479, which had been employed on shunting work at Newhaven, survived to become the last active E4 Class engine in the area. No.32479 departed for Eastleigh on 1st June, so ending the long association of this class with Brighton. *W.G. Sumner/Les Dench collection*

One of the most absorbing locations for steam power on the SR during the period covered by this album was undoubtedly Brighton where, even as late as mid-1962, an assortment of types could be observed. These ranged from the little Stroudley A1X Class 0-6-0Ts to both rebuilt and un-rebuilt Bulleid Pacifics and a number of BR Standard Class 4MT 2-6-4Ts. At this time Brighton shed had a very generous total of nine Bulleid Pacifics allocated and these were primarily employed on inter-regional trains via Salisbury, and Oxted Line duties. At the end of 1962 there was a massive purge of steam locomotives for accounting reasons on the SR and this included all remaining E6 Class 0-6-2Ts, K Class 'Moguls' and 'Schools' Class 4-4-0 locomotives. In the Brighton area the engines affected were dumped in sidings at Hove and on 29th December 1962 Nos.30901/11/15/23, 32338/41/2 and 32417/8/74/79 were congregated there. Some of the locomotives were still in steam, having been at work only a few hours previously. It is thought that the last E4 Class engines were meant to have been included in the mass withdrawal programme but, due to a shortage of motive power caused by a prolonged spell of bitterly cold weather, Nos.32468 and 32503 remained at work. Fate overtook No.32468 on 8th January, however, when it got out of control approaching Kemp Town whilst powering the 8.00am goods from Brighton and crashed into the buffer stops. Though not extensively damaged it was withdrawn from traffic. Four days later, due to the continuing shortage of power, sister locomotives Nos.32474/79 were resurrected from the dump and returned to work. The former was sent to Three Bridges shed, which used it on passenger services to East Grinstead, whilst No.32479 was despatched to Newhaven. During March No.32474 was working regularly from Norwood Junction shed, but its brief reprieve ended on 11th May when it left 'light engine' on its final journey to Eastleigh for scrapping. It is seen here passing Norwood Junction on 16th March 1963. *W.G. Sumner/Les Dench collection*

On 12th April 1963 the line up of withdrawn locomotives presented a truly melancholy sight with most of the engines still in quite presentable external condition. Nearest to the camera is U1 Class No.31895 while the engine next to it appears to be K Class 'Mogul' No.32341, followed by No.32468, the engine whose career came to an abrupt end at Kemp Town. The composition of the dump had obviously undergone several changes since the first engines arrived. The steam scene at Brighton suffered another blow at the end of the 1963 summer timetable when all of the depot's stud of Bulleid Pacifics was transferred away as a result of the mass invasion of diesels. At least local enthusiasts had a crumb of compensation in that the Brighton to Plymouth train was henceforth worked by an Exmouth Junction Pacific and during the first fortnight of the new arrangements a total of nine different locomotives appeared. *Michael Chown*

During October 1961 centenary celebrations took place on the Steyning Line, these including the appearance of specially cleaned E4 Class No.32468, complete with a small headboard, on two return trains. The former Brighton Works 'Terrier' No.32635, in Stroudley yellow livery, was on display in the goods yard at Steyning where the station was decorated for the occasion. By the time this picture of the 9.30am *ex*-Brighton was taken at West Grinstead on 4th May 1963, however, the days of 'Brighton' motive power on the line were well and truly over and most services were in the hands of Ivatt 2-6-2Ts or BR Standard Class 4MT 2-6-4Ts. Exactly a year later, on 4th May 1964, the Brighton to Horsham service was completely dieselised using units surplus from the Hampshire lines. Note the clean condition of No.41303 indicating that it was, of course, a Brighton-based engine. *Michael Chown*

The end of steam on the Horsham trains in early May 1964 meant that Brighton shed's last local duties for steam traction ended, apart from the Lancing workmen's train, known locally as the 'Lancing Belle'. Brighton shed, however, continued to supply locomotives to its sub depot of Three Bridges, but this arrangement proved to be very short lived. The shed closed from 15th June 1964, after which date the 'Belle' was diesel hauled, but the pace of change was so rapid that it ran for the last time on 3rd July, an ordinary electric train being provided in its place. At the end of June the only occupants of Brighton shed were two condemned Ivatt 2-6-2Ts, Nos.41326/7 (which departed for scrapping at Kettering during August) and, incredibly, an intruder from the LMR, Stanier Class 6P5F 'Jubilee' 4-6-0 No.45672 *Anson*. The latter had been dumped there after failing on the Newhaven to Stirling car-sleeper on 21st June and eventually left for Willesden travelling at slow speed on 2nd July. Actually the 'Jubilee', which was apparently only the third member of its class ever to reach Brighton, should never have been allowed down the Brighton main line in the first place: presumably somebody on the LMR mistook it for a 'Black Five'! After the end of local steam working at Brighton, Eastbourne shed became the focal point for servicing purposes, but most of its visitors were 'foreign' locomotives from other regions. Interestingly, Eastbourne still had a modicum of local steam working on 'Cuckoo Line' trains. In this picture Ivatt 2-6-2T No.41260 awaits departure from Brighton with the 'Lancing Belle' on 20th May 1964, just a few weeks before the curtain came down for good on regular steam working in the area. *Les Dench*

The old order on the Waterloo to Exeter line! A down Salisbury to Exeter stopping train, with Bulleid 'Battle of Britain' Pacific No.34064 *Fighter Command* in charge, pauses at Axminster on 14th May 1960. Note that at the time of this photograph the locomotive still retained the old-style BR emblem on its tender. No.34064 was later experimentally fitted with a Giesel ejector in a somewhat belated effort to improve efficiency and reduce the cost of running steam traction. There were a number of stopping trains west of Salisbury which were timed to provide connections out of fast expresses, but they were probably rather expensive to operate. In this case the locomotive and tender weighed much more than the three coaches forming the train. *John Langford*

WR DIESELS REPLACE STEAM ON THE WATERLOO TO EXETER LINE

The SR was well known for a number of named trains, among them the 'Golden Arrow' and the 'Brighton Belle' but, surely, the most famous of them all was the multi-portioned 'Atlantic Coast Express' that ran from Waterloo to the west of England. The 'Atlantic Coast Express', or 'ACE' as it was referred to colloquially, was inaugurated in July 1926 and ran for many years with 'King Arthur' Class engines as its staple motive power. The train was suspended during the Second World War, but when it resumed operation in May 1946 its appearance was totally transformed, with handsome Bulleid coaches hauled by one of the same designer's legendary 'Pacifics' replacing the Maunsell stock previously employed. By the early 1960s the 'ACE' had the most demanding schedule of any train in Great Britain that was regularly operated by steam traction and was booked to cover the 83-mile section between Waterloo and Salisbury in 80 min. In this evocative picture No.35029 *Ellerman Lines,* complete with a prominent 'Atlantic Coast Express' headboard, nears Honiton tunnel with the up train on 4th August 1962, with the rolling Devon hills providing the perfect backcloth. Note the huge pile of coal in the tender which appears to be out of gauge. The last booked, up steam-hauled 'ACE' beyond Exeter ran on 14th August 1964 following the introduction of a small number of 'Warship' Class diesels on the Waterloo to West of England main line, but the down train remained a rostered steam turn until the end of the summer timetable, by which time the full complement of diesels was available. The final weekday service was powered by immaculately turned-out No.35022 *Holland America Line* which ran like an engine possessed to Salisbury, the run being completed in 78 min. Beyond there the performance was equally noteworthy, 90mph being attained before Templecombe. The 'ACE' certainly went out on a high note! *John Beckett*

Many passengers and enthusiasts had considerable misgivings when it was announced that the Western Region was to take over all SR lines west of Salisbury (Wilton South) from 1st January 1963. There was much debate at the time about the future of so-called duplicate routes and it seemed unlikely that the WR would choose to develop the Waterloo–West of England line in preference to its own route from Paddington via Taunton. Various timetable changes in the early 1960s had steadily reduced the number of portions conveyed by the 'ACE' so, to some degree, the rot had already set in, but worse, much worse, was yet to come. It was announced that from 7th September 1964 a revised diesel-hauled, semi-fast service of five weekday trains was to be introduced on the Waterloo–West of England route and that trains would run to and from Exeter only and would no longer convey through portions to the small towns in Devon/Cornwall which had been such a hallmark of the SR's operation. The most savage development in the minds of many people, however, was the fact that the 'ACE', probably the busiest train of the day, was to be replaced by a Waterloo to Salisbury service and passengers travelling further west would be forced to change at Salisbury onto the Brighton to Plymouth train. Overnight the SR's flagship route was to be downgraded to little more than a secondary line and it was widely felt that the rival WR was determined to starve the SR route of as much traffic as possible as a prelude to closure. Exeter Central station was the hub of operations in the west where main line expresses normally changed engines, while coaches were being divided or added before resuming the journey. In this shot Bulleid 'West Country' Class No.34107 *Blandford Forum*, at the head of an unidentified London-bound express, waits in the up main platform, perhaps while another portion is added onto the rear of its train. This picture was taken in August 1964 which was the last full month of traditional operations on the Waterloo to West of England main line before the dieselisation and a drastic reduction of services took place. *Colin Caddy*

WR DIESELS REPLACE STEAM ON THE WATERLOO TO EXETER LINE

The 'Atlantic Coast Express' on enemy territory!
In order to reach Southern tracks east of Exeter trains from Cornwall and North Devon had to run over a short section of former GWR line. Here Bulleid Pacific No.34066 *Spitfire* is seen 'blowing off ' in St Davids station with the up 'ACE' on 2nd September 1964, during this famous express's last week of operation. The lower quadrant signals in the foreground conclusively prove the origins of this line. At that time Exeter St Davids was a particularly confusing station for travellers because trains to the same destination (London or Plymouth) could leave in opposite directions. This still applies today for London-bound services. *Les Dench*

The station running-in board that says it all! Change at Sidmouth Junction for the rest of the world – well, almost. The 1.10pm Exeter Central to Salisbury stopping train, hauled by 'Battle of Britain' Class Pacific No.34059 *Sir Archibald Sinclair* runs into Sidmouth Junction station, also on 2nd September 1964. Once again, the weight of the locomotive exceeded that of the coaches and vans it was pulling. Some of the stopping trains on this line could scarcely be described as 'speedy' because in the summer 1957 timetable this service took three hours to cover the 88 miles between those points. No.34059 turned out to be quite a lucky locomotive because, following withdrawal in May 1966, it was sent to Woodham Bros. scrap yard at Barry docks in South Wales. It lay there for many years until rescue came in 1979 when it was purchased by a small group of enthusiasts and transported to the Bluebell Railway for restoration to working order. It is possible that this may have been achieved by the time this album is published. *Les Dench*

Oh dear, what a depressing sight! Rebuilt 'Light Pacific' No.34093 *Saunton*, which is caked in a thick layer of grime, coasts downhill from Honiton tunnel with an unidentified eastbound train on 5th September 1964. Trains travelling in the up direction faced a considerable climb from Sidmouth Junction which, after a short section on a favourable gradient, entailed climbing over four miles at 1 in 100 or thereabouts. The incline steepened to 1 in 90 before the summit, this being located just inside the western end of Honiton tunnel. In the down direction the ascent was even more formidable, involving six miles of climbing at mostly 1 in 80, a stern test for the firemen of heavy holiday expresses. The last booked steam-hauled train down from Waterloo was the 4.00pm express the following day which reportedly had No.34109 *Sir Trafford Leigh-Mallory* in charge. The poor reliability of the replacement diesels ensured that steam continued to put in regular appearances, however, and there were even some steam diagrams on summer Saturday additional trains during 1965. *Roy Hobbs*

After steam was largely banished from the section west of Salisbury, one or two odd workings remained including the 6.10pm Salisbury to Yeovil Junction passenger train, the locomotive of which returned on the 8.23pm Yeovil to Waterloo vans. East of Salisbury, steam traction continued to see regular use on a variety of duties, the most noteworthy being the few services to and from Waterloo during the peaks. Remarkably, some of these were booked for steam until July 1967. In this illustration BR Standard Class 5MT 4-6-0 No.73065, in surprisingly clean condition, approaches Grateley with a down train on a clear and bright 22nd January 1967. *David Clark*

The small town of Midhurst was originally served by three routes, to Chichester, Petersfield and Pulborough, but none of these lightly used lines was economically viable. The line to Chichester, which traversed a very sparsely populated rural area, was closed to passengers way back in 1935 and had the dubious distinction of being one of the first routes of any consequence to be closed by the erstwhile Southern Railway. The cross-country link from Petersfield to Pulborough only served, apart from Midhurst, a few scattered villages in a very quiet rural area. It was closed to passengers from 7th February 1955, the section west of Midhurst closing completely. In this exceptionally rare colour photograph of the line, a train to Pulborough is seen waiting to leave Petersfield on a rather gloomy 29th January 1955 with an unidentified LSWR M7 Class locomotive in charge. In the early days of this line branch trains used the up loop platform at the main station which was just across the road behind the photographer, but eventually the shelterless bay platform seen here was brought into use and apparently deemed to be adequate. The single line to Midhurst is the left hand track of the two lines under the bridge; the other track served a rubber works. *Neil Davenport*

The section of line between Pulborough and Midhurst stayed open for goods traffic and, not unnaturally, attracted one or two enthusiasts' specials at various times. A Locomotive Club of Great Britain rail tour, hauled by LBSCR E4 Class No.32503 piloting E6 Class No. 32417 leaves Selham on 24th June 1962. The rural nature of this route is apparent from this picture. The final train left Midhurst in October 1964, whilst Petworth kept its rail connection for a little longer, not closing until 20th May 1966.
Alan Chandler

DECLINE AND FALL OF THE MIDHURST BRANCHES

The LSWR T9 Class 4-4-0s were, in the author's opinion, one of the most attractive and elegant locomotive designs ever to work in the south of England. At the end of 1960 a total of fourteen of these machines were still in traffic, but not all were operational. Most of the class was concentrated in the West Country for use on the North Cornwall Line, but at least one or two, including No.30707, could be seen working a variety of turns around the Eastleigh area, a particular favourite being the 10.57am Salisbury to Portsmouth van train. By mid-May 1961 the number of working engines at Okehampton was down to three, Nos. 30120, 30313 and 30709, and all of these engines finished regular work a few weeks later. They arrived at Eastleigh during June and were subsequently withdrawn from service, apart from No.30120 which had been selected for official preservation by the Curator of Historical Relics. This is a lucky locomotive, because Nos.30117 and 30288 had been considered for preservation, but rejected owing to their poor condition. No.120 (as No.30120 had become) received a comprehensive overhaul at Eastleigh Works, emerging resplendent in LSWR colours in late March 1962, and was immediately put to work on local duties, including passenger turns such as the Portsmouth portion of the Brighton to Plymouth through train. It was, almost needless to say, used on some rail tours, the first being in June 1962. At one time No.120 had a regular turn on the 12.42pm SO Waterloo to Basingstoke local train which is pictured passing Vauxhall on a very wet 14th July 1962. No.120 was retired from regular use in July 1963 and later spent long periods in store at various locations before returning to steam, in lined BR black livery, on the Mid Hants Railway in May 1983. At the time of writing it is based at the Bluebell Railway, but is not currently operational. *David Wigley*

THE RESTORATION OF T9 CLASS NO. 30120 TO LSWR LIVERY

During the twilight years of steam traction on the SR Eastleigh Works was responsible for heavy and intermediate overhauls of steam locomotives but, as the end of steam approached, the scope of the work being undertaken was gradually reduced. Towards the end only light repairs were carried out in order to keep a minimum number of locomotives operational and the last scheduled work was undertaken in October 1966. This involved Bulleid 'Battle of Britain' Pacific No.34089 *602 Squadron* which was ceremonially outshopped on 6th October. Television cameras were present to record the event and several staff were interviewed. No.34066 *Spitfire* is seen receiving attention in the works in July 1966. *Roy Hobbs*

A view of the little-photographed locomotive shed (or what was left of it!) at Eastbourne on 13th June 1965. The locomotives are Maunsell 'Mogul' No.31803, which had presumably just been turned after working in with a rail tour, and BR Standard Class 4MT No.80084. The tour marked the end of regular steam working on the Central Division and by implication the end of Eastbourne shed. The ruins seen here are actually the remains of the third shed in Eastbourne. The first dated from the opening of the railway in 1849, but that was superseded by a roundhouse, built adjacent to the station, in 1876. The third shed opened in 1912 on a site some distance from the station, whereupon the roundhouse was closed. Following the closure of Brighton shed in June 1964, Eastbourne shed became the main servicing point in the area for steam traction and was visited by a fair number of 'foreign' locomotives that had reached the Sussex coast on inter-regional workings. These were mainly 'Class Fives' of both BR Standard and Stanier varieties but, remarkably, LMSR 'Jubilee' 4-6-0s and a LNER-designed B1 4-6-0 were also observed. *Alan Chandler*

MAINTAINING THE FLEET

A partial view of Feltham shed seen on a snowy day in February 1965 with BR Standard Class 5MT No.73082 *Camelot* prominent in the picture. The six-road through shed here was completed in 1923 and was the first major locomotive shed on the Southern to be constructed of concrete. Feltham's towering 200-ton coaling plant, clearly visible on the left, was a product of the Mitchell Conveyor & Transporter Co. Ltd. and it should be noted that the wagon hoist and tipping area are enclosed in corrugated cladding in an attempt to minimise coal dust. Feltham was primarily a freight shed and was renowned for its allocation of large freight tank engines. The depot was officially closed to steam at the end of 1966, but in reality it continued to play host to the occasional visiting steam engine right up to the end of SR steam in July 1967. *Neil Davenport*

The lower quadrant signals on the right give an immediate clue as to the location of this photograph. It is, of course, Reading Southern shed, officially known as Reading South, and it was latterly a sub-shed of Guildford. The shed appears to be a veritable hive of activity in this picture with a number of locomotives looking as though they are about to move off the shed at any minute. Perhaps they were, but the shot gives a somewhat misleading impression, because this picture was taken on the last Saturday of steam working on the Reading to Redhill line, 2nd January 1965, and such scenes were soon to be consigned to history. It is thought that there had been a depot on this site since about 1853, but today no trace of the premises remain, the site having been completely redeveloped. *David Wigley*

Southern steam in the West Country as it will always be remembered. Maunsell N Class 'Mogul' No.31834 crosses the girder bridge at Little Petherick Creek, between Wadebridge and Padstow, with an afternoon train from Bodmin North to Padstow on 6th June 1961. Many railway photographs have been taken over the years at this truly delightful spot, where a hill provided a grandstand view of approaching trains. Passenger trains between the two Cornish towns ceased to run from 30th January 1967 and the bridge no longer echoes to the sound of trains passing over its spans. The structure remains in use, however, as part of the 'Camel Trail' public footpath. *John Beckett*

Dugald Drummond's T9 Class 4-4-0s were surely among the most elegant and well-proportioned locomotives ever built. Sixty-six of these machines were constructed between 1899 and 1901 for express passenger duties and due to their free-steaming capabilities they were often referred to by enginemen as 'Greyhounds'. The T9s were largely displaced by more modern engines in the 1920s but were modified and took on a new role as secondary express locomotives. In this portrait No.30313, a Nine Elms product dating from September 1901, is seen near Old Town Cove, just over a mile or so from the end of the line at Padstow, with a westbound mixed train on 13th June 1961. In theory, thirteen of these handsome engines were still in traffic at the start of 1961 but some were stored unserviceable and others only saw occasional use. Apart from Nos.30117 and 30707, which were still in sporadic use at Eastleigh, the last remaining active examples were all based at Exmouth Junction shed for working the North Cornwall Line. By the beginning of July all of the last five survivors, Nos.30120, 30313, 30709/15/7, had arrived at Eastleigh Works and were withdrawn later the same month, except for the first mentioned which was retained for special traffic purposes. Who knows, perhaps the 13th June 1961 was No.30313's last day in service! *John Beckett*

The end of the line from Waterloo! Even without the prominent running-in board Padstow station would probably be quickly recognised by most readers as the location of this picture. Ivatt-designed Class 2MT 2-6-2T No.41275, which is in quite presentable external condition, simmers in the platform with the 8.12am train to Bodmin General on 1st June 1963. In the summer 1957 timetable the 'Atlantic Coast Express' was booked to reach Padstow, 259¾ miles from Waterloo, in exactly six hours, of which the journey beyond Exeter occupied nearly three hours. *Alan Chandler*

The same locomotive is seen again, this time passing Dunmere Junction with the 9.50am Wadebridge to Bodmin North train. The tiny signal cabin, visible on the left of the picture, controlled the junction with the freight only branch to Wenford Bridge which can be seen diverging from the 'main line' on the right. No.41275 was built at Crewe in October 1950 and remained in service until October 1965. It spent most of its BR career at Bletchley shed before being moved to the West Country. *Alan Chandler*

Halwill Junction was a pleasant country junction station where nothing happened for hours and then, all of a sudden, there would be a feverish bout of activity when inter-connecting trains arrived from all directions almost simultaneously. Calm was restored once they had gone on their way. It is likely, however, that the appearance of Bulleid 'West Country' Class Pacific No.34020 *Seaton* with an up freight working on 1st June 1963 was timed to coincide with a lull in activity. 1963 proved to be No.34020's last full year in traffic because when the WR reorganised services on the Waterloo to Exeter line in September 1964 it inherited a number of Bulleid Pacifics which were declared to be 'surplus to requirements'. Some were transferred to the SR for further use but No.34020 was among a batch of eleven that was immediately withdrawn from service. *Alan Chandler*

Maunsell N Class 'Mogul' No.31840 crosses the river Taw at Barnstaple with the 9.5am Ilfracombe to Exeter train on 2nd June 1963. The unusual curving bridge, which connected Barnstaple Junction and Town stations, was a favourite haunt of railway photographers and many pictures must have been taken there over the years. The Ilfracombe line was especially busy with holiday trains on summer Saturdays, but the provision of rolling stock in order to meet peak summer demand was deemed to be uneconomic by the late Doctor (later Lord) Beeching and many dated holiday trains quickly disappeared from the timetables. An additional handicap for the line was the inconvenient location of Ilfracombe station in relation to the town and, consequently, the branch withered, the last trains running in October 1970. *Alan Chandler*

The line between Barnstaple and Ilfracombe was characterised by extremely steep gradients, the line climbing at 1 in 40 or steeper in both directions to a 600ft-high summit at Mortehoe station. Heavy trains required banking assistance as far as Mortehoe and the signalman there must have been busy on summer Saturdays when holiday traffic was at its height. In this portrait an Exeter to Ilfracombe train, headed by Bulleid 'West Country' Class Pacific No.34020 *Seaton,* appears to be taking the 1 in 40 incline up to Mortehoe station in its stride. This picture was taken on 18th June 1963. *John Beckett*

Opposite: The 2.00pm Barnstaple Junction to Torrington train, formed of WR stock and headed by Ivatt Class 2MT 2-6-2T No.41313, accelerates away from Fremington and heads for its next station stop at Instow on a somewhat overcast 21st June 1963. Note the rather fine elevated signal box which is just visible on Fremington station in the distance. In times gone by the adjacent quay was very busy handling coal, timber and china clay and 50,000 tons of the first-mentioned commodity were sometimes imported in a single year. Much of the coal was for railway use at the Exeter district engine sheds. The quay was closed in March 1970. The passenger service between Barnstaple Junction and Torrington was withdrawn from 4th October 1965 but the line remained opened for china clay traffic from Meeth until September 1982. *John Beckett*

The idyllic estuary of the river Camel provides a hint of the beautiful landscape in this part of Cornwall as Maunsell N Class 'Mogul' No.31843 shunts stock at Padstow on 10th June 1964. During the following six months the traditional Southern flavour of the lines in this part of Cornwall, by this time firmly under WR control, was almost completely eradicated. The 'Atlantic Coast Express' ran for the last time at the end of the summer timetable on 5th September and during the ensuing months SR motive power was replaced by BR Standard types on those lines west of Exeter that remained steam worked. Steam traction on the North Cornwall and Bude lines came to an end from 4th January 1965 when diesel units took over. This resulted in enginemen at Bude, Launceston and Wadebridge being declared redundant. Padstow lost its passenger trains from 30th January 1967 when services on the link to Bodmin Road ended. *John Beckett*

The 6.00pm Padstow to Okehampton train, hauled by Maunsell N Class 'Mogul' No.31853 and formed of only two coaches and a van, has just emerged from Trelill tunnel, between St Kew Highway and Port Isaac Road stations, on 19th June 1964. This 62 miles-long line traversed one of the most lightly populated areas in the south-west of England and must have been highly unremunerative from BR's point of view but, needless to say, it was much loved by railway aficionados and its loss is still mourned by many today. When the service was taken over by diesel units in January 1965 only four trains were provided each way on weekdays and some of these were formed of single unit railcars. It is recorded that trains sometimes ran completely empty. The end came on 3rd October 1966 when passenger trains were withdrawn from the Wadebridge to Okehampton section and this lovely route faded into history. *John Beckett*

The up 'Atlantic Coast Express', headed by Bulleid 'Battle of Britain' Class Pacific No.34066 *Spitfire,* awaits departure from Okehampton on 2nd September 1964. This everyday scene had been repeated many times over the years but not for much longer, because the shot was taken during this famous train's final week of operation. The wholesale dieselisation of the Southern routes around Exeter from 7th September 1964 resulted, as previously mentioned, in many locomotives becoming redundant and a fair number were withdrawn. No.34066 was one of the lucky ones, however, and found itself transferred back to the SR and allocated to Salisbury shed. It was eventually withdrawn in September 1966. *Les Dench*

SOUTHERN STEAM'S LAST STAND IN THE WEST COUNTRY

The cross-country route from Redhill to Reading ran through some really attractive countryside, especially between Reigate and Guildford, where it followed the escarpment of the North Downs. In days gone by, long distance inter-regional trains from the Kent coast to the north of England used to come this way, a routing that involved a time consuming reversal at Redhill. Former GWR locomotives were frequently visitors to Redhill on these plus other services, in addition to a considerable variety of other SR types. These included the lovely LSWR T9 Class 4-4-0s, and Maunsell S15 Class 4-6-0s, a number of which were based at Redhill for freight purposes. The line was, perhaps, best known for the fact that towards the end of SR steam traction it was one of the last strongholds of the Maunsell 'Moguls' on passenger working. In October 1964, for example, all of the remaining 23 locomotives of this type were based at either Redhill or Guildford sheds. Here, No.31864 is seen leaving Betchworth with a westbound train on 27th July 1963. *David Clark*

REDHILL TO READING – THE LAST STRONGHOLD OF THE MAUNSELL 'MOGULS'

The 27th of July 1963 seems to have been a popular day with railway photographers intent on photographing the Redhill to Reading line, because here is another shot taken on the same day! In this gem of a picture, bales of hay dot the fields in the foreground on (what appears to have been) a wonderful summer's evening as an unidentified Maunsell 'Mogul', hauling a three-coach set of Bulleid stock, gets into its stride after its stop at Dorking Town station with the 7.09pm Redhill to Reading train. It is difficult to believe that such a peaceful and beautiful area is only 20 miles from the centre of London. *Michael Chown*

The face of the well-known comedienne Dora Bryan looks out on this everyday scene at Guildford as Maunsell N Class 'Mogul' No.31866 waits to resume its journey with the 6.09pm Redhill to Reading train on 16th May 1964. Note the track on which the train is standing: it is one of the few examples in this country with a platform on both sides. This particularly fascinating feature of Guildford station still survives today, but not with such interesting motive power, alas! Built at Ashford in May 1925, No.31866 lasted in traffic until January 1966. *Alan Chandler*

Maunsell U Class 'Mogul' No.31809 makes a quick getaway from Blackwater with a Reading-bound train which is formed of a set of three Bulleid coaches. This picture was taken on 10th October 1964. The attractive, brightly painted signal box on the left is in stark contrast to the rather dirty locomotive. *David Wigley*

Between Guildford and Reading the nature of the line was markedly different to the stretch west of Reigate because it passed through much more densely populated areas, one of these being Farnborough. In this shot U Class 'Mogul' No.31790 eases away from Farnborough North station with a Redhill-bound working, also on 10th October 1964. This engine was originally constructed for the SECR as the prototype 'River' Class 2-6-4T at Ashford Works in 1917 and was named *River Avon*. It was the only example of the 'River' Class to run in SECR days, but more engines were built in the mid-1920s. Following complaints of bad riding and several derailments, all of the 'River' Class locomotives were rebuilt, becoming U Class tender engines, this particular locomotive being converted in 1928. *David Wigley*

The 11.05am train from Reading to Redhill, in charge of BR Standard Class 4MT 2-6-0 No.76031, has just diverged from the Portsmouth Direct Line, the course of which can just be discerned between the trees, passed over the River Wey on the girder bridge and approaches Shalford station on 17th October 1964. At the date of this photograph SR trains still used Reading Southern station, but this was closed and services diverted to the former Reading General from 6th September 1965. Whilst the majority of trains on this route were hauled by Maunsell 'Moguls', some produced other motive power as evidenced by this shot. No.76031 spent much of its career on the Eastern Region, initially at Stratford shed and later at March, before moving to the SR in late 1962. It was based at Brighton for a while and then moved to Guildford, where it was still active until steam traction was abolished on the SR in July 1967. *John Beckett*

The 3rd of January 1965 was a very sad date for Southern steam enthusiasts because it was the final day of rostered steam traction on the Redhill to Reading line and, indeed, the Redhill to Tonbridge line as well. Yet another nail firmly hammered into steam traction's coffin! An hourly diesel service, supplemented by diesel locomotive-hauled trains at peak times, was scheduled to come into operation the following day. The previous month had been a rewarding one for observers at Redhill due to the large number of Christmas mails and parcels trains being run, and some double-heading was noted on the Reading line, including the 4.04pm Redhill to Reading which produced BR Standard Class 5MT No.73113 *Lyonnesse* piloting N Class No.31831 on 22nd December. Two days before BR Standard Class 9F 2-10-0 No.92241 had steamed into Redhill at the head of a special freight from Reading. During the last weekend of steam working it was appropriate that Maunsell 'Moguls' dominated, a total of eleven different engines being recorded during the two days. On Sunday 3rd January services were in the hands of three 'Moguls', Nos. 31809/16/62, and two BR Standard engines. In this shot No.31816 coasts into Gomshall and Shere with the 12.32pm from Redhill to Reading on the penultimate day of steam operation. *Alan Chandler*

Photographed on 12th October 1963, the 11.12am Redhill to Tonbridge train, hauled by Maunsell U Class No.31620, passes Crowhurst Junction South. At one time this link formed the South Eastern Railway's southern access to the Croydon and Oxted Joint line, but it ceased to be used regularly in May 1955. It continued in sporadic use for weekend diversions and seasonal excursion traffic for the next five years or so, being especially busy at hop-picking time. Such workings had practically ended by the early 1960s, however, and the line fell into disuse. It was officially closed from October 1965, the last known working being an enthusiasts' special on 3rd January 1965. This picture was taken from the signal box steps: note the lower quadrant signal above the second carriage of the train. *Michael Chown*

A Redhill to Tonbridge train, with BR Standard 2-6-4T No.80140 in charge, is seen leaving Redhill in 1964, the last full year of regular steam working between the two towns. There is a stiff initial climb away from Redhill for trains heading east, but after that the gradients are favourable. The steam workings on this line were dieselised in January 1965 as part of the Redhill to Reading scheme. During the final week of steam working some excitement was caused by the appearance of Bulleid Q1 Class 0-6-0 No.33006 on a passenger train. On Sunday 3rd January various BR Standard 2-6-4Ts from Tonbridge were noted running westwards 'light engine' and one train, the 10.45am Tonbridge to Redhill, had double-headed 2-6-4Ts in the shape of Nos.80068 and 80089 hauling seven coaches and a van. Obviously the operating authorities were having a 'clear out' prior to the start of diesel working the following day. Tonbridge shed had been officially closed (and lost its allocation) way back in June 1962, but it stayed open for stabling steam locomotives used on the Redhill and Eridge lines until January 1965, thus becoming steam's last stronghold in Kent. *John Beckett*

STEAM FINISHES ON THE REDHILL TO TONBRIDGE LINE

Maunsell's Q Class 0-6-0s, which were introduced to replace some of the ageing engines of the same type that the Southern Railway inherited, are unlikely to go down in history as his most successful design. They were notoriously poor steamers until Bulleid fitted them with multiple-jet blastpipes and large diameter chimneys. The class was one of the last designs of 0-6-0 tender engines to appear in Great Britain and a total of twenty was constructed at Eastleigh in 1938/39. Withdrawals commenced in December 1962 and continued until April 1965 when the last two survivors, Nos.30535 and 30545, were taken out of traffic. Judging by the paucity of pictures submitted for this album the engines were rather camera-shy even bearing in mind the small number of locomotives in the class. Here, a nicely cleaned No.30530 takes the joint LCGB/RCTS 'Midhurst Belle' rail tour through Selham on the way back from Midhurst on 18th October 1964. This was the last passenger train to reach the Sussex town. *David Wigley*

The original railway system in the county of Surrey is almost intact and almost survived the notorious Beeching era unscathed. This is, of course, due to its close proximity to London and heavy commuter traffic. The delightful Horsham to Guildford line was an exception to this rule, however, and fell victim to the late Doctor (later Lord) Beeching's infamous axe in June 1965. This robbed the south of England of one of its prettiest and most unspoilt branch lines which had a tranquil and relaxing atmosphere all of its own. Perhaps the most well-known station on the line was Baynards, where the station staff cultivated a riotous display of dahlias to occupy their time during the long gaps between trains. The flowers lined the platforms and visitors came from far and wide to admire them but, unfortunately, the vast majority arrived by car! One wonders how many purchased a platform ticket. Strictly speaking, this vintage picture, taken on 10th October 1953, of LBSCR C2X Class 0-6-0 No.32444 simmering in Baynards station's down platform with the daily freight, is outside the scope of this book, but who could possibly resist including such a gem? The C2X Class engines were originally built as C2 Class but later rebuilt with larger boilers and re-classified. No.32444 dated from June 1893 and was withdrawn in March 1960. The class became extinct in February 1962 when the final survivors were taken out of service and subsequently scrapped. *Neil Davenport*

THE HORSHAM TO GUILDFORD BRANCH

Photographed back in the days when Doctor Richard Beeching was yet to become a household name and private motoring was still very much the preserve of the better off, a Horsham to Guildford train pauses at Baynards station on 10th October 1953. Motive power is nicely cleaned M7 Class 0-4-4T No.30047, a Horsham-based engine. The train just visible in the distance beyond the signal is a goods train with a C2X Class locomotive at its head, which is depicted in the previous illustration. *Neil Davenport*

The Horsham to Guildford line was almost exclusively steam operated during its closing years and therefore widely photographed, but there are no prizes for guessing which station was the favourite with photographers. In this picture a Guildford to Horsham train waits at Baynards and, once again, the photographer has managed to get at least some of the famous blooms into the shot. This portrait was taken on 19th October 1963 and the motive power is Ivatt-designed Class 2MT 2-6-2T No.41287, a class of locomotive that was very common on the route towards the end. The train in the background on the left appears to be the daily goods, with a Bulleid Q1 Class 0-6-0 in charge. Baynards was very popular with film-makers. *David Wigley*

A Bulleid Q1 Class 0-6-0, No.33012, makes an energetic getaway from Cranleigh with a train bound for Horsham on 10th October 1964. The end came for this idyllic backwater when it was closed completely from 14th June 1965, the last timetabled trains running on 12th June because there was no Sunday service. However, an enthusiasts' special ran on 13th June and was powered over the Horsham to Guildford line by a brace of Q1 Class engines, Nos.33006 and 33027, that had been spruced up for the occasion. The end of this route, coupled with the closure of the 'Cuckoo Line' the same weekend, resulted in the virtual extinction of regular steam working in Sussex. *David Wigley*

Lovely countryside, steep gradients and attractive, substantially-built stations were the hallmarks of the much-loved and lamented 'Cuckoo Line' that ran from Eridge to Polegate. Much of the steam operation over this highly scenic route was curtailed by the widespread introduction of diesel units on the East Sussex routes and towards the end steam workings were largely covered by BR Standard Class 4MT 2-6-4Ts, although sometimes a Maunsell 'Mogul' appeared on the odd turn. This picture, which shows the 6.52am Tunbridge Wells West to Eastbourne train pausing at Horam on 22nd May 1965 with BR Standard 2-6-4T No.80084 in charge, is a typical scene from the last days of this line. The line north of Hailsham closed to passenger traffic from 14th June 1965, the final timetabled steam working being the 9.00am Eastbourne to Tunbridge Wells train on 12th June powered by No.80141. Later the same day a six-coach BR-sponsored excursion from Eastbourne to Tunbridge Wells and back was hauled by sister engine No.80144 and, apparently, was very well supported. Wreaths were ceremonially attached to the engine at Mayfield on the return journey. The following day an enthusiasts' special traversed the line during a comprehensive tour of Sussex branch lines. That weekend (as previously mentioned) effectively marked the end of regular steam operation in the county and the shed at Redhill was closed together with its sub-depots of Eastbourne, Three Bridges and Tunbridge Wells. *Michael Chown*

CLOSURE OF THE 'CUCKOO LINE' – THE END OF A TRULY OUTSTANDING ROUTE

A commendably clean SECR H Class 0-4-4T, No.31544, makes a fine sight in the morning sunshine as it hurries along a thickly wooded section of line between Three Bridges and Rowfant. It was working the 11.08am from Three Bridges to East Grinstead on 7th October 1962. At this time an hourly service was provided on weekdays on this line and good connections were generally available with main line services at Three Bridges.
Alan Chandler

The 1.27pm East Grinstead to Three Bridges train, with LSWR M7 Class 0-4-4T No.30053 in charge, pulls out of East Grinstead High Level station on a snowy 22nd January 1963. Following its displacement from this line shortly after this picture was taken, No.30053 was moved to Bournemouth depot to bolster that shed's allocation of M7s which were reported to be thoroughly worn out and in need of replacement. In the event, however, the class soldiered on until June 1964 by which time they were confined to duties on the Lymington and Swanage branches. No.30053 miraculously appeared on a rail tour in the London area in early July 1964 and was later purchased for private preservation. In 1967 it was shipped to the Steamtown Railway Museum in Vermont, U.S.A., certainly the longest journey the M7 ever undertook! After twenty years in the United States, No.30053 was acquired by the 'Southern Repatriation Group' and returned to Great Britain for use on the delightful Swanage branch in Dorset. *John Beckett*

THREE BRIDGES TO EAST GRINSTEAD – A SUSSEX BYWAY

A fine portrait of SECR H Class 0-4-4T No.31544 standing in Rowfant station with a Three Bridges to East Grinstead train on 8th April 1963. The tail lamp on the front of the engine indicates that the locomotive is propelling, the stock in this case being two Maunsell carriages that have been converted for push-pull operation. These engines were constructed between 1904 and 1915, No.31544 being one of the first examples to be built. It first saw the light of day at Ashford Works in November 1904 and was equipped for push-pull operation in June 1954. No.31544 was withdrawn from service in September 1963. *David Clark*

Rowfant station is the location of this shot of LSWR M7 Class 0-4-4T No.30055 propelling an East Grinstead to Three Bridges 'push-pull' train on 27th April 1963. At the beginning of 1963 a total of seven of these locomotives were available for this service, at least in theory, but all of them were withdrawn or transferred elsewhere during that year. No.30055, which was built at Nine Elms and entered service in December 1905, was withdrawn in September 1963. *David Clark*

The 2.27pm service to Three Bridges, with H Class No.31518 in charge, stands in East Grinstead (High Level) station on 26th May 1963. East Grinstead station is, arguably, the most interesting station depicted in this album. It was a 'double decker' station, the upper section being served by London/Three Bridges to Tunbridge Wells services whilst the lower platforms were used by trains on the Lewes line and terminating London trains. The low level platforms appear to have been disused at the time of this photograph (note the rusty rail surfaces) but were subsequently restored to use when the Three Bridges to Tunbridge Wells West service was withdrawn. The first railway to reach the town was the branch from Three Bridges that was opened in 1855 but the station was on a different site to that seen here. When this line was extended to Tunbridge Wells in 1866 another station was commissioned in a different position from the first one. The premises seen here were constructed when the line from Lewes reached East Grinstead in 1882, this being on a further different site. Shortly after this picture was taken the run-down of steam traction on this line commenced in earnest, most off-peak steam workings being eliminated from 17th June. Tunbridge Wells West shed was closed as an independent depot on 9th September (but retained servicing facilities), and Three Bridges depot suffered complete closure on 6th January 1964, the last three remaining H Class tank engines, No.31263 and 31518/51 being withdrawn from that date. Henceforth, the very modest steam motive power requirements for the Three Bridges to East Grinstead line were supplied by Brighton shed until it, too, was closed and, later, Redhill. Steam working of a few peak hour services, using BR Standard Class 4MT 2-6-4Ts, continued on the line until June 1965.
John Beckett

Over the years many pictures of Bulleid Pacifics climbing out of Weymouth on passenger workings have been published, but here is something a little different. The train seen here is a freight, comprised of oil tank and barrier wagons, and motive power is an unidentified Maunsell S15 4-6-0. This shot was taken on 13th September 1962. The S15 Class locomotives were built in two principal batches, Nos.30496 to 30515 being constructed to Urie's original LSWR design whilst Nos.30823 to 30847 were a development of the first series of locomotives and built during the Maunsell era. The first batch was built in 1920/21, while the second series was constructed during a nine-year period from 1927 to 1936. Locomotives in the later series had a higher boiler pressure than the original engines and other detail differences: Nos.30833 to 30837, for example, were equipped with six-wheel tenders for working on the Central Section. *John Beckett*

THE MAUNSELL S15s GO OUT IN A BLAZE OF GLORY

The widespread introduction of BRCW Type 3 diesel locomotives, coupled with a fall in the amount of goods traffic being conveyed by BR, made many S15 Class engines redundant and the final members of the class, Nos.30824/37/8/9/42, were withdrawn from Feltham shed in September 1965. The Locomotive Club of Great Britain, which obviously had considerable influence in the high echelons of the SR headquarters at Waterloo, decided to run an S15 Class commemorative rail tour for which No.30837 was specially retained, despite the fact that it had been officially withdrawn from service. In addition to being kept on one side, the locomotive was polished to perfection by the staff at Feltham, the buffer beams repainted and many fittings burnished. In the event the tour was substantially over-subscribed and a relief to the main event, which was scheduled for 16th January 1966, was run a week earlier. No.30837 presented a truly magnificent spectacle when it worked the first trip on 9th January and most participants agreed that it was one of the most memorable sights they had ever seen. It is illustrated here tackling Medstead Bank, south of Alton, in fine style with the relief tour, marking the demise of this distinctive class. *Charles Whetmath*

During the following few days the weather throughout the south of England turned very cold and by the time the second train ran, on 16th January 1966, the landscape was carpeted in deep snow. In view of the weather conditions, and no doubt as a precaution against further heavy snowfalls, it was decided to provide an assisting locomotive for the heavily graded Alton to Eastleigh section of the tour. This was U Class 'Mogul' No.31639, which had hauled the train over the Bentley to Bordon branch, and the pair are seen here doing battle with the 1 in 60 climb between Alton and Medstead. This was the third consecutive weekend that No.31639 had been on rail tour duty. There is no doubt that these tours provided an immense amount of enjoyment for many people but, very sadly, No.30837 later went for scrap and perhaps it would have been better in the long term if all of the participants had donated their fares towards the locomotive's preservation. *Charles Whetmath*

'Downright ugly' would probably be most enthusiasts' description of Bulleid's Q1 Class 0-6-0s and photographers often turned their camera away when one of these engines hove into view. Consequently, very few shots of these locomotives were offered for publication in this album. If there was ever a competition to find the 'most shunned locomotives in Great Britain' the Q1s would surely be runaway winners. This is a great pity, bearing in mind they performed the tough job they were designed for quite brilliantly and in the author's view were certainly Bulleid's most successful design. They were built in response to a desperate wartime need for a very powerful locomotive with wide route availability and as a result the highly unconventional Q1s were devoid of many traditional features such as running plates, splashers and orthodox boiler cladding. This not only reduced their weight but also saved precious materials. Their BFB (Bulleid Firth Brown) 'Boxpok' wheels added to their really weird appearance. Withdrawals commenced in 1963 and such was the rate of condemnations that by December 1964 only seven were left in traffic. Three examples, Nos.33006/20/27, survived into 1966 all working from Guildford shed, principally on ballast duties. Even the bright, sunny conditions fail to make No.33026 look attractive as it poses at Three Bridges shed in September 1962. Built at Ashford in July 1942, this example worked until September 1965. *Roy Hobbs*

BULLEID'S Q1 CLASS 0-6-0s BOW OUT

Despite their apparent unpopularity with enthusiasts some Q1s actually appeared on rail tours, so perhaps it was the case that affection for the class rose as their numbers decreased. By the time the LCGB 'Wealdsman' tour ran on 13th June 1965, the Q1 Class was down to only six survivors which were employed principally on unpredictable freight plus ballast duties and it is likely that much of their line work was at night-time. So, perhaps, it was not surprising when Nos.33006 and 33027 were booked to haul the tour over its last stage from Horsham to Guildford via Cranleigh and then to Waterloo via Cobham. The class had worked regularly over the Horsham to Guildford line on freight, and the occasional passenger train, for some time and was therefore appropriate to the route. Here they are seen heading towards Baynards tunnel with the 'Wealdsman' tour which was the very last train over the line. The numberplate of the leading engine has been altered to read 'C27', this being the original Southern Railway number for the locomotive. *Roy Hobbs*

It is a commonly held belief that the S&D became vulnerable to closure when the Western Region (WR) assumed control of the line north of Henstridge in 1958 (excluding Templecombe station which remained with the SR). Later the WR gained control of a further section southwards to Blandford Forum and also the entire Waterloo to Exeter line west of Salisbury. The writing was on the wall for the line when, in September 1962, the 'Pines Express' and all other through trains between the North of England, the Midlands and Bournemouth were diverted to travel over other routes. No attempt was made by BR to improve the timetable or introduce more economical diesel traction and, amazingly, some services whose main purpose was to connect with the 'Pines Express' were left in the timetable and consequently ran almost empty! The WR also diverted traditional freight traffic flows away from the line, such as the Avonmouth to Blandford Forum fertilizer trains which were sent on a huge detour via Westbury, Salisbury and Southampton (135 miles rather than 65!) solely to deprive the S&D of this traffic. In this photograph, taken during the final summer of through inter-regional trains, former S&D Class 7F 2-8-0 No.53806 approaches Midsomer Norton South station with the 7.35am Nottingham to Bournemouth West train on 18th August 1962. The S&D was a highly individualistic route with a special identity all of its own and staff took an immense pride in their line, as evidenced here by the beautifully arranged flower bed adjacent to the station platform.
Les Dench

In addition to some really glorious scenery the S&D also ran through the Somerset coalfield with its unsightly heaps of colliery waste and pithead gear, which were totally alien to a county noted for the beauty of its countryside – a real blot on the landscape! In this illustration the 10.05am Bournemouth West to Bradford train, double-headed by BR Standard 4-6-0 No.75073 and Bulleid 'West Country' Class No.34043 *Combe Martin*, is depicted passing Norton Hill colliery, near Midsomer Norton, also on 18th August 1962. No.34043 later became one of the first Bulleid Pacifics to be withdrawn. It was a regular performer on the S&D and constant 'hammering' over the line's very heavy gradients no doubt took its toll. *Les Dench*

The 'Pines Express', which ran from Bournemouth to Manchester, was undoubtedly the best-known train to operate along the S&D line and in this portrait BR Standard Class 9F No.92233 approaches Broadstone with the northbound working. This shot was taken on 7th September 1962, the train's penultimate day of operation on the S&D line. The 9Fs were introduced on the S&D route following trials in March 1960 and it is fair to say that they transformed operation of the route's heavy summer holiday traffic, being permitted to take 410 tons unassisted. No.92233 was one of four engines of this class allocated to Bath (Green Park) shed during the summer of 1962. *John Beckett*

The climb over the Mendip Hills from Radstock to Masbury summit involved eight miles of climbing, much of it at a gradient of 1 in 50. In this illustration former S&D Class 7F 2-8-0 No.53808 toils up the 1 in 53 (not quite so steep!) between Midsomer Norton and Chilcompton with the 2.00pm goods train from Bath to Templecombe on 12th September 1962. The twin bore Chilcompton tunnel, from which the train is emerging, is a reminder that the Bath Extension, as the line north of Evercreech Junction was originally known, was constructed as two single lines.
John Beckett

No.53808 is seen again, this time on rail tour duty for which it has obviously been given special attention by the cleaners at Bath Green Park shed. This picture shows the locomotive hauling the LCGB's 'Somerset & Dorset Rail Tour' at Cannards Grave, near Shepton Mallet, on 30th September 1962. The trip had a marvellous itinerary, starting at London Waterloo and traversing the Brockenhurst to Ringwood line in order to reach Broadstone, from where No.53808 powered the train as far as Evercreech Junction. On arrival there the participants travelled along the Highbridge branch and return. They were lucky enough to traverse the little-used section to Burnham-on-Sea which was a rare treat and, for some of the passengers at least, probably the highlight of the day. On arrival back at Evercreech the train continued to Bath, with No.53808 in charge once again. It eventually returned to London Paddington with Great Western motive power which included a 'County' Class 4-6-0.
John Beckett

Southbound trains from Bath (Green Park) faced a very difficult 2½ miles-long climb out of the city. This involved the passage of Devonshire tunnel, a very restricted single-line bore, and after a slow, laborious climb through the smoky tunnel enginemen must have experienced a tremendous feeling of relief when their train at last emerged into the fresh air of Lyncombe Vale, which was located between Devonshire and Combe Down tunnels. In this picture, which was taken on 30th March 1964, BR Standard Class 5MT No.73051, in quite clean condition, climbs the 1 in 50 gradient through Lyncombe Vale and approaches Combe Down tunnel. The summit of the climb was just inside the northern end of this tunnel and marked the start of the descent towards Midford. The train is passing over Watery Bottom Bridge (officially bridge No.12) that carried the line over Lyn stream. *Michael Chown*

A beautiful pastoral scene about a mile north of Wincanton, showing BR Standard Class 5MT No.73051 drifting along effortlessly with the 1.10pm Bath to Templecombe train on 11th July 1964. Note the milk tank wagons, conveying milk from Bason Bridge on the Highbridge branch, which would have been attached at Evercreech Junction. The year 1964 was a particularly significant one in the more recent history of the S&D because during that year the WR hammered another nail into the line's coffin by withdrawing the night-time freight workings. Consequently, the line was closed at night for the first time. The Stanier Class 5MT locomotives, and their BR Standard derivatives, were universally liked on the S&D and this example was one of the batch allocated to Bath shed when brand-new in May 1954. Sadly, No.73051 was withdrawn in August 1965 and scrapped three months later. *Michael Chown*

In 1964 a change of government took place and the incoming Labour administration stated that no further railway closures would be approved until a co-ordinated transport policy had been formulated. It must have come as a dreadful shock to staff on the S&D line to learn during 1965 that their hopes had been dashed and the route had been sanctioned for closure. The withdrawal of services was originally due to take place on 3rd January 1966 but there were problems with replacement bus services and, much to the embarrassment of the WR which had unwisely proclaimed it would dispense with steam traction from that date, a much reduced service ran for another two months. So, the S&D was forced to carry on, thus prolonging the agony until the bus services could be sorted out. Here, on 1st January 1966, which would have been the last day for the S&D if BR's plans had not gone awry, BR Standard Class 5MT No.73001, in absolutely diabolical condition, drifts into Stalbridge with the 9.00am Bristol Temple Meads to Bournemouth train. *Alan Chandler*

The 2.18pm to Templecombe sets off from Highbridge on 1st January 1966 behind Ivatt Class 2MT 2-6-2T No.41296, a type that had latterly monopolised Highbridge branch workings. When the S&D was first built, remarkably its 'main line' ran from Wimborne, in Dorset, to Burnham-on-Sea. Highbridge was the location of the S&D's locomotive and rolling stock repair works and about 300 men were employed there prior to its closure in 1930. The buildings were still extant, however, at the time of the line's closure. The line continued beyond Highbridge to Burnham-on-Sea, crossing the GWR main Bristol to Taunton line on the level but the line to Burnham was closed to regular traffic in 1951. Towards the end, the Highbridge branch was very lightly used and the S&D section of Highbridge Station came to resemble something of a ghost station served by a handful of poorly patronised trains. On reflection, perhaps it was something of a miracle that this delightful backwater lasted for so long. *Alan Chandler*

An 'Interim Emergency Service' was introduced on the line from 3rd January 1966 which advertised only four trains on weekdays between Evercreech Junction and Bath and a mere two weekday trains on the Highbridge branch. The service south of Templecombe was better but could hardly be described as lavish. The line's infrastructure had been systematically destroyed over a long period, with goods yards and signal boxes closed, and most stations had not been repainted for years so it probably came as a relief to staff when the line was finally laid to rest on the evening of 6th March 1966 after the last of the special trains had gone. The 5th of March had been the final day of public services and here the last 8.15am Bath to Templecombe train, hauled by Stanier 8F Class 2-8-0 No.48760, climbs towards Masbury summit, between Chilcompton and Binegar. The 8F would have been unable to supply heating to the train but most of the passengers were probably 'last day' revellers, so who cared? *Michael Chown*

The last public train to leave Bath (Green Park) in daylight was the 4.25pm 'all stations' service to Templecombe on 5th March 1966, which was formed of a 3-coach set of Bulleid designed stock hauled by BR Standard 2-6-4T No.80043. Later the same evening No.80043 piloted sister locomotive No.80041 back to Bath with the last up passenger train, the 8.20pm from Templecombe. In this shot No.80043 is seen crossing Midford viaduct in glorious late afternoon sunshine. The engine carried a small 'Farewell S&D' headboard in addition to the S&D coat-of-arms affixed to the middle lamp bracket to commemorate this extremely melancholy occasion. The tiny building just visible towards the rear of the train is Midford signal box which was rebuilt with a sloping flat roof following an accident in July 1936. *Michael Chown*

In this superb panoramic picture a brace of BR Standard Class 4MT 2-6-4Ts, Nos. 80134 and 80146, take a trainload of army vehicles past Spetisbury on 22nd July 1966. The S&D had, of course, been closed to passengers by this date, but the section from Broadstone to Blandford Forum was kept open for freight traffic. It is interesting to note that the photographer, who was simply visiting the area, had no prior knowledge of this working and happened to discover the two locomotives standing in Blandford Forum station. Naturally he made enquiries to find out what was happening, and when he was told that the train was due to depart he immediately set off down the line to find a suitable photographic location and this absorbing picture resulted. There used to be a station at Spetisbury, which opened on 1st November 1860, but it never prospered and was reduced in status to an unstaffed halt in August 1934. It closed completely on 17th September 1956. *David Wigley*

The last few years of steam on the SR were, to put it mildly, depressing for steam fans. The deplorable mechanical condition of many locomotives was only too apparent from their lacklustre performances, whilst externally most engines were caked in thick layers of grime and never seemed to be cleaned, apart from when they were called upon to work a special. All was not quite doom and gloom, however, and one of the highlights of the final years were the regular booked weekend diversions due to extensive engineering operations on the main Waterloo to Bournemouth line. They took steam traction over steeply graded routes that were usually entirely operated by modern motive power and were consequently of great interest to the enthusiast fraternity. Here an unidentified Bulleid Pacific takes a London-bound train across the bridge at Bursledon on 20th March 1966, a day when services were being diverted via the Portsmouth Direct line. *Michael Chown*

The BR Standard classes were generally quite noisy machines and one can only imagine the deafening sound being produced by Class 5MT No.73114 *Etarre* as it shatters the peace of the Hampshire countryside, also on 20th March 1966. This train is seen on the challenging 1 in 80 climb from Rowlands Castle to Buriton tunnel from where the enginemen would have been able to relax as their train sped down towards Petersfield. After passing there the line climbs once again virtually all of the way to Haslemere so the crew's period of relaxation would have been brief. *Michael Chown*

The extremely steeply graded Alton to Winchester line also saw a large number of diverted trains due to the main line being closed for trackwork. This route was one of the most difficult to operate on the SR because of its long climbs in each direction up to a summit at Medstead & Four Marks station which is situated at an altitude of 652 feet above sea level, the highest point on any line in the south of England. Unfortunately, there were a number of cases when locomotives in a parlous condition stalled on the 1 in 60 climb while working overnight trains from London. On 18th September 1966, for example, BR Standard Class 5MT No.73083 *Pendragon* reportedly took 54 minutes to complete the climb from Alton to Medstead while working the 2.55am Waterloo to Poole newspaper train and this 'record' time included three stops for a 'blow up' to raise steam. BR faced severe criticism of the delays to overnight trains from the Newspaper Publishers Association and subsequently rostered a 'Warship' Class diesel locomotive in an attempt to improve matters, but this move backfired because, on the first day of the new arrangements, it failed at Butts Junction and had to be rescued by a steam locomotive! On another notorious occasion the Southampton football team was delayed when No.34023 *Blackmore Vale* slipped to a stand on Medstead Bank whilst powering the 10.35pm *ex*-Waterloo. This prompted the comment from a BR spokesman that only locomotives in the best condition were rostered to work the overnight services! In this picture, which was taken on 24th April 1966, Bulleid Pacific No.34060 *25 Squadron* appears to be making a confident ascent of Medstead Bank with the 10.30am Waterloo to Weymouth in tow. *Roy Hobbs*

In this, another picture taken on 24th April 1966, the down 'Bournemouth Belle' is seen climbing the bank towards Medstead with BRCW 1,550hp Type 3 (later Class 33) No.D6556 assisting Bulleid 'West Country' Pacific No.34017 *Ilfracombe*. The diesel locomotive was attached at Alton. The main A31 road, which runs parallel to the railway at this point, is partially concealed by trees in the foreground. *Charles Whetmath*

On 15th May 1966 it was the turn of some up services to be diverted along the Alton to Winchester line and in this portrait a very smart looking Bulleid 'Battle of Britain' Class, No.34059 *Sir Archibald Sinclair*, takes the 10.34am Bournemouth to Waterloo through Ropley station. This station is famous for its topiary and some examples of this can just be discerned on the station platform in the background. This stretch of line is now owned by the Mid Hants Railway whose locomotive works now occupy the land in the foreground so it is not possible to take this picture today. *Sir Archibald Sinclair* was rescued for preservation at the Bluebell Railway and is now nearing the end of a thorough restoration from scrap yard condition, and may have returned to steam by the time this book is published. *Charles Whetmath*

Most railway photographers have had frustrating experiences, when a potentially stunning photograph was ruined by a small cloud blotting out the sun at the wrong moment or the locomotive's exhaust steam blowing down and obscuring the train. But, once in a while, everything turns out perfectly as seen here in this masterpiece of a photograph which shows Bulleid Pacific No.34101 *Hartland* at Tunnel Hill, between Pirbright Junction and Ash Vale. The photographer has pressed the camera shutter at precisely the right time, so that the engine is in sun, whilst luck has also played a part because a second or two later the electric train would have completely spoiled the picture. The train in view is the 4.30pm from Waterloo to Weymouth and this shot was taken on 12th June 1966. *Charles Whetmath*

The Maunsell 'Moguls' could reasonably be described as 'maids of all work' that were an everyday sight on most parts of the SR system, from Kent to Cornwall. There were two principal classes, the N Class and the U Class, plus their three cylinder versions, the N1 and U1 classes. Construction of the 'Moguls' started in 1917 when No.810 (later No.31810) appeared from Ashford Works and continued for no less than seventeen years, the last locomotive to be built being No.1414 (later No.31414) which was out-shopped at Ashford in January 1934. A total of 157 of these sturdy and reliable machines was eventually built. The menacing, dark clouds indicate that a storm was brewing at Battledown flyover on 21st July 1962 as No.31638 speeds past with a sizeable down van train in tow. *Michael Chown*

Opposite above: The River Test bridge, just west of Southampton, is the location of this picture of U Class No.31809 with 11.53am Eastleigh to Bournemouth train which, rather curiously, is formed of GWR coaches. This shot was taken on 4th August 1962. No.31809 was rebuilt at Brighton Works from a K Class 2-6-4T following the Sevenoaks accident on 27th August 1927. In this accident K Class 2-6-4T No.800 *River Cray* was derailed at speed with disastrous results. At the inquiry it was found that track defects were largely to blame for the derailment but it also emerged that the K Class engines (also known as the 'River' Class) tended to be unstable at speed and a decision was subsequently taken to rebuild the entire class as 2-6-0 tender engines. No.31809, formerly No.809 *River Dart,* lasted in service until January 1966. *Michael Chown*

Opposite below: Towards the end of their careers the Maunsell 'Moguls' were generally relegated to ballast train working in connection with the Bournemouth line electrification and in this photograph No.31639 is seen on such a working at Surbiton on 15th May 1966, about a month before its withdrawal from traffic. Their last stronghold on passenger work was the Reading to Tonbridge line (which is featured elsewhere in this book) but during 1965 representatives of both the N and U classes could still be discovered on a variety of other passenger services, provided one knew where to look, of course! During the early months of 1965 the 7.00am Reading to Southampton Terminus train was a regular duty for a Maunsell 'Mogul' south of Basingstoke, whilst the 4.10pm Southampton Terminus to Bournemouth stopping train also produced one of these locomotives on a regular basis. Until the end of the 1964-1965 winter timetable an engine of this type was often rostered for the 6.40pm Bournemouth to Woking train. The last passenger train that was sometimes worked by a 'Mogul' was the 7.30am Woking to Basingstoke but this was taken over by WR diesel units from 16th May 1966. The last Maunsell 'Moguls' in traffic, all allocated to Guildford shed, were Nos.31405/8, 31639 and 31791 and these were officially withdrawn during June 1966, so this celebrated design just missed its fiftieth birthday. *Charles Whetmath*

TIME RUNS OUT FOR THE LAST MAUNSELL 'MOGULS'

One of the highlights of 1966 for steam enthusiasts in the south of England was the visit of A4 Class No.60024 *Kingfisher,* which worked two rail tours in March. This locomotive, one of Sir Nigel Gresley's legendary streamlined Pacifics, was one of only five survivors still working in Scotland on the three-hour trains between Glasgow and Aberdeen. The engine was based at the latter location so it would be something of an understatement to say that it had a long journey to reach the SR! On Saturday 26th March No.60024 powered an A4 Preservation Society special from Waterloo to Weymouth and back, while the following day, after spending the night at Nine Elms shed, it was in action on a more demanding assignment working a Locomotive Club of Great Britain special from Waterloo to Exeter and return. Surprisingly, this was not the first time a member of the A4 class had visited the West Country because No.60022 *Mallard* powered a similar train on 24th February 1963 and returned up the GWR main line to Paddington which was rather novel. During

its layover at Exeter No.60024 retired to Exmouth Junction shed and is seen here emitting clouds of black smoke whilst a member of the train crew does a spot of oiling. By this time regular steam working at Exeter had become a thing of the past so, presumably, a special supply of coal had to be obtained to replenish *Kingfisher*'s tender. Unlike the previous special train, No.60024 returned to London via Salisbury … *David Wigley*

… and after completing the run from Exeter watched by hundreds of lineside spectators and photographers, *Kingfisher* takes water amid the unaccustomed surroundings of Salisbury station. The exploits of No.60024 sparked a great deal of interest among the railway enthusiast community as evidenced here by the number of people at the end of the platform. Many of the staff employed in the engine diagrams section of the South Western Division's Wimbledon headquarters were steam fans and they had apparently laid plans for No.60024 to leave the SR in style on a revenue earning service rather than 'light engine'. The idea was for *Kingfisher* to work the 10.30am from Waterloo to Weymouth as far as Bournemouth on 28th March and then take the following day's northbound 'Pines Express'. Unfortunately, the locomotive failed with a collapsed brick arch and these imaginative plans were thwarted. What a pity! *David Wigley*

For reasons unknown to the author most of the 'foreign' engines that visited the SR for rail tour duty were of LNER design. Perhaps it was because locomotives of GWR or LMSR origin sometimes worked on SR metals in normal service and therefore were not considered to be sufficiently 'different' or 'exciting' to warrant consideration. Another reason was that certain GWR classes were out of gauge and, therefore, were not permitted on to SR metals. Some of the rail tour organisers' plans did not always come to fruition, however, perhaps the worst case being the LCGB's 'Green Arrow' trip proposed for 3rd July 1966, the booked engine of which suffered a whole series of misfortunes and the trip degenerated into a total fiasco. The locomotive earmarked for the tour was No.60919, one of the last survivors still in service at Dundee (Tay Bridge) shed at this time. It left Scotland on 25th June but on the morning of the tour was failed at Nine Elms shed with a broken spring. It was patched up and left for Eastleigh with the intention that it

would take over the special train from No.34002 *Salisbury* which had been substituted at the last minute. On arrival there one of No.60919's injectors was proving temperamental and the traffic control wisely decided that it was a total liability and sent it back to London, but even this arrangement was thwarted when the V2 failed at Basingstoke with an overheated bearing! At least the participants, who had the compensation of a brilliant performance by *Salisbury,* caught a fleeting glimpse of the disgraced V2 Class locomotive sitting in Basingstoke shed yard. In this picture No.60919 is seen lurking in the depths of Nine Elms shed on the day before the tour. *Roger Cruse*

The LCGB were obviously not too downhearted by their experience with No.60919 and no doubt hoped that an unprecedented visit by A2 Class No.60532 *Blue Peter* would erase the memory of their misfortune. Alas, it was not to be, because the 'A2 Commemorative Rail Tour' of 14th August 1966 also turned out to be an almost unmitigated disaster. The crew were obviously ill-at-ease with their unaccustomed mount and, after an undistinguished run from Waterloo, Exeter was reached no less that two hours in arrears. A cylinder cock was apparently jammed open throughout the journey as evidenced here by the escaping steam at the locomotive's front end. Efforts were made to rebuild *Blue Peter*'s fire and this appeared to have a beneficial effect during the run to Westbury but, even so, arrival there was a massive three hours late. BR Standard 'Britannia' Pacific No.70004 *William Shakespeare* had been booked to haul the train the short distance to Salisbury, while the A2 went ahead to be turned and serviced, but in the event it was decreed that, in view of the lateness, No.70004 would carry on through to Waterloo. During its visit in March 1966, No.60024 *Kingfisher* had run like the wind but, regrettably, the ensuing visitors from Scotland had hardly run at all. Here, No.60532 is depicted limping away from Salisbury with its cylinder cocks emitting clouds of steam. *Michael Chown*

Horse meets iron horse at Corfe Castle! A horse grazing in a field adjacent to Corfe Castle station does not give LSWR M7 Class 0-4-4T No.30379 a second glance as it shuffles by with a train for Swanage on 30th September 1962. M7s are understood to have been used on the branch since the 1940s but by the date of this picture most representatives of this class were reported to be in poor mechanical condition, which appears to be borne out by the amount of steam leaking from No.30379's cylinders. The M7s lasted for almost another two years, however, being replaced completely on the branch in May 1964, a move which doubtless met with the unanimous approval of enginemen. No.30379 was almost sixty years old when this shot was taken and lasted until October 1963.
John Beckett

Photographed on the sunny summer's evening of 2nd July 1966, an anonymous BR Standard Class 4MT 2-6-4T locomotive makes an energetic departure from Swanage with the 5.00pm train to Wareham. At the time of this photograph the branch service consisted of fourteen trains in each direction on weekdays so there were plenty of trains to keep any visiting photographers happy! An evening weekday rush-hour train down the branch started from Bournemouth, but all of the remaining services started or terminated their journeys at Wareham. An interesting aspect of operations on the branch was that trains crossed at Corfe Castle but when the line was dieselised it was worked by a single unit, so this practice ceased. Note the rather attractive bracket signal, the lower signal arm of which controlled access to the goods yard. *Charles Whetmath*

THE SWANAGE BRANCH'S PASSENGER TRAINS ARE DIESELISED

The distant outline of the remains of Corfe Castle provide an unmistakable backdrop to this shot of tender-first BR Standard Class 4MT 2-6-0 No.76014 puffing gently down the branch to Swanage with the 6.30pm departure from Wareham, which was formed of a very modest load. This scene was recorded on 3rd July 1966, on a beautiful summer's evening. The castle was an important stronghold during the time of William the Conqueror, but the Class 4MT locomotive was of much more recent origin. No.76014 was built at Horwich Works, Lancashire, in February 1953 and lasted in traffic for only a further two months after this shot was taken. *Charles Whetmath*

THE SWANAGE BRANCH'S PASSENGER TRAINS ARE DIESELISED

Most visitors to the Isle of Wight go for its warm summer temperatures, beautiful sandy beaches and unspoilt countryside. But in the mid-1960s the island was the regular haunt of hordes of railway enthusiasts who came to experience another of the island's undoubted attractions – its Victorian railway system where steam was still king. The Isle of Wight's isolation from the mainland meant that it was not possible to easily draft in more modern motive power to replace the ageing and increasingly unreliable LSWR O2 Class 0-4-4Ts that had latterly been the mainstay of the traffic department. This picture was taken on 2nd October 1957 when the O2 Class engines were still in relatively fine fettle and shows an immaculate No.W14 *Fishbourne* between the Pier Head and Esplanade stations at Ryde with a train to Cowes. Note the elderly, pre-grouping carriages forming the train which remained in use on the island long after they had disappeared from services on the mainland. *Neil Davenport*

GOODBYE TO VINTAGE STEAM ON THE ISLE OF WIGHT

Could this be the most photographed telephone booth in the Isle of Wight? It certainly seemed to be in a rather precarious position on the edge of the platform, but probably proved a godsend for visiting holiday-makers who wished to call a taxi to take them to their hotel. The location is, of course, Ventnor station and in this shot the crew are seen 'watering' O2 Class No.W17 *Seaview* after arrival with a train from Ryde on 4th May 1958. Many of the lines on the island served sparsely populated areas and were totally unremunerative from BR's point of view, the first closures taking place in the early 1950s. The line to Ventnor lasted considerably longer, the section beyond Shanklin not closing until April 1966. *Neil Davenport*

A colourful row of motor coaches lines the waterfront near Ryde Esplanade station as an unidentified O2 Class locomotive, hauling a train bound for Cowes, is about to enter the tunnel that takes the railway beneath the town and onto the next station at St John's Road. The awnings of Ryde Esplanade station can just be discerned above the last coach of the train. This picture was taken on 16th August 1964, at the height of the holiday season when the railway's locomotive and rolling stock resources would have been stretched to their limit. The tunnel is below the level of high tides and consequently prone to flooding. In order to prevent such a calamity pumps are housed in the building on the left of the shot. *David Wigley*

Photographed in glorious sunshine for which the Isle of Wight is so renowned, O2 Class 0-4-4T No.W28 *Ashey* emits a superb smoke effect just as the photographer is about to click the shutter. The locomotive's fireman could not have timed it better! It was powering the 12.10pm Ryde Pier Head to Ventnor train near Shanklin on 26th June 1965. Between August 1864 and September 1866 Shanklin was the terminus of the line from Ryde. It is, of course, a terminus once again following the closure of the line onwards to Ventnor. No.W28 was built in July 1890 and survived right to the end of steam hauled passenger services on the island in December 1966. *John Beckett*

A scene at Newport on 21st August 1965 depicting the 3.35pm Ryde Pier Head to Cowes train pulling out of the station with O2 Class No.W20 *Shanklin* in charge. Once the hub of the island's railway system, with routes fanning out to Freshwater, Sandown and Ventnor, by the time of this picture only the Ryde to Cowes line remained. This lasted until 21st February 1966, when the final passenger trains ran. When steam traction had ceased completely on the island all of the remaining locomotives (with the exception of No.W24 *Calbourne* which was earmarked for private preservation) were moved to Newport for cutting-up, which became a graveyard for steam traction. *Alan Chandler*

The extinction of regular steam working on the island at the end of December 1966 was an extremely sad event and passenger receipts, which had been boosted by enthusiasts' fares, no doubt suffered a sharp downturn after that date. On the final day, 31st December, the island witnessed a mass invasion and every enthusiast in the south of England worthy of the name seemed to be present, such were the crowds on that day. To commemorate the demise of steam the LCGB ran a 'Vectis Farewell' rail tour which was powered by Nos.W24 *Calbourne* and W31 *Chale* between Ryde and Shanklin and return, this being all that remained of the once extensive network on the island. The outward journey was made in very dull conditions, but by the time the train left Shanklin on the return trip the sun was shining brightly out of a clear blue sky, which hopefully raised the spirits of the gathered multitude just a little! The train is seen here near Brading. Double-heading was a very rare occurrence on the Isle of Wight, so this picture is of considerable historical interest. *Roger Cruse*

While the vast majority of people present on the Isle of Wight to witness the last day of steam were capturing the final moments on film, the well-known artist David Shepherd was, naturally, using an altogether different medium. He is seen here at work amidst piles of clinker at Ryde shed on that fateful day. The subject of his painting is No.W27 *Merstone*, which was apparently the last engine to steam under BR auspicies and the first of the survivors to be broken-up at Newport. By the date of this picture the staff at Ryde had, understandably, lost much of their interest in the job and many of the locomotives were in grubby condition, as seen here. No.W14 *Fishbourne*, on the right, is suitably adorned with a small headboard and wreath. The end of an era indeed. *John Beckett*

GOODBYE TO VINTAGE STEAM ON THE ISLE OF WIGHT

The Southern Region, like nearly all other areas of Great Britain, had a substantial number of branch lines, but by 1967 the Lymington branch was the only one remaining on the SR with a steam-worked passenger service. Indeed, by that time it had become the *very last* branch in Great Britain with steam-operated passenger trains, although it should be pointed out that various goods-only branches in other parts of the country continued to be steam-worked. For many years the line was virtually the sole preserve of the faithful LSWR M7 Class 0-4-4Ts, but they were replaced by more modern Ivatt Class 2MT 2-6-2Ts, supplemented by BR Standard Class 4MT 2-6-4Ts, in 1964. Naturally during the last few weeks of steam traction enthusiasts flocked to this distinctive part of Hampshire to ride behind and photograph steam engines at work on the branch's regular passenger trains. One wonders what the line's regular commuters made of it all! Here, in this view taken on 25th March 1967, a number of enthusiasts are clearly in evidence as No.80134 awaits departure from Lymington Pier station. *David Wigley*

BROCKENHURST TO LYMINGTON – THE LAST STEAM PASSENGER BRANCH

Onlookers are transfixed as Ivatt 2-6-2T No.41320 pulls away from Lymington Pier station on 26th March 1967 in brilliant late afternoon lighting conditions. Judging by the road surface it had been raining earlier in the day but, fortunately for the photographer, the sun emerged just at the right time. Railway photography can be an absolutely frustrating and infuriating pastime when the reverse happens, but on this occasion the photographer had luck on his side. *Roger Cruse*

Most pictures of trains on the Lymington branch appear to be confined to static shots taken at either Brockenhurst, the main line junction station in the heart of the New Forest, or either of the two stations at Lymington. But, for a change, here is an action photograph, depicting No.80152 working the 1.15pm Lymington Pier to Brockenhurst train on 1st April 1967. For reasons unknown to the author the engine is not carrying the headboard seen in the previous pictures. Two days later diesel units ousted steam traction, but they were simply a short term replacement until electrification occurred in July. The branch remains operational and at the time of writing is once again a source of interest to enthusiasts as the last outpost of slam-door electric stock. *Alan Chandler*

For passengers wishing to travel to Southampton or Bournemouth in style, the 'Bournemouth Belle' offered the last word in luxury, elegance and service. The train's opulent and spacious Pullman cars, where meals were served at every seat and patrons cosseted throughout the journey, provided far superior accommodation to anything available on the ordinary timetabled services. The 'Belle', as it was known to railway staff, first ran in July 1931, initially on every Sunday throughout the year and daily during the summer period. All-year-round daily operation commenced in January 1936 and the usual motive power at that time was a Maunsell 'Lord Nelson' Class 4-6-0. The train ceased running during the Second World War, but resumed operation after the cessation of hostilities. By this time Bulleid's highly distinctive 'Merchant Navy' Class Pacifics were in general use and locomotives of this class were assigned to work the 'Belle'. These engines must have been a very impressive sight at the head of a train of immaculate Pullman cars and doubtless lifted the spirits of many people during the grim, immediate post-war years which were marked by food and fuel shortages. Supplements were payable for travel in the Pullman cars and in 1957 the second class supplement from Waterloo to Southampton was two shillings and sixpence (12½p), while the extra charge for Bournemouth passengers was four shillings (20p): first class fares were around 50% higher. The 'Bournemouth Belle' was regularly rostered for Bulleid Pacifics until January 1967 when Brush Type 4 (later Class 47) diesels theoretically took over, but in practice steam traction frequently deputised and even during the last week of Southern steam a number of substitutions were noted. The last recorded steam appearances were on 5th July 1967 when No.34024 *Tamar Valley* took the down train, the 12.30pm from Waterloo, while No.34036 *Westward Ho* hauled the up working, at 4.37pm from Bournemouth. Perhaps, if BR had been really smart they could have got away with charging an extra supplement when the 'Belle' was steam-hauled. Regrettably, towards the end many staff had, understandably, lost some of their pride and dedication and the 'Belle' was often marred by a dirty engine, as seen here. The location is Deepcut cutting, between Brookwood and Farnborough, and this picture was taken on 7th May 1966. The motive power is thought to be 'West Country' Pacific No.34004 *Yeovil*. *Charles Whetmath*

Photographed against a beautiful display of autumn colours, BR Standard Class 4MT 2-6-0 No.76062 passes Ascot West with a long freight train in tow. This picture was taken on 7th November 1964. This locomotive was fitted with a BR1B 4,725 gallon tender which had a much higher water capacity than other types of tender fitted to this class of locomotive. Ascot West was not open for regular passenger traffic but was used when race meetings were being held at the nearby Ascot racecourse. In addition, it served the base of the well-known Bertram Mills circus whose stock was stabled nearby. Presumably, elephants and other circus animals regularly used the platforms there! *David Wigley*

Just after the end of the Second World War the Southern Railway purchased fourteen American-built 0-6-0Ts, that were stored as war surplus material, to replace their ageing fleet of B4 Class dock tanks. The locomotives, which were purchased at a bargain price, were overhauled at Eastleigh and they entered service in 1947 as the USA Class. They were put to work on shunting duties at Southampton docks, employment to which they were ideally suited. The entire class was based at a shed within the docks area and No.30064, which was in appalling external condition at that time, was photographed there some time in the late 1950s. In 1962 the class was replaced by an identical number of purpose-built diesel shunters, but many of the USA Class engines were in good condition and found new roles employed as departmental shunters at various locations. Some of them were repainted in SR green prior to taking up their new duties. No.30064 was repaired and repainted at Eastleigh Works in February 1964 but, unlike some other members of the class, it retained its original BR running number. No.30064 stayed at Eastleigh for a time, where it was usually used as the locomotive works' shunter, but finished its days as Guildford shed pilot. It continued in service until the end of steam on the SR and can be seen, at the time of writing, on the Bluebell Railway. *Ken Wightman/David Clark collection*

THE USA CLASS TANKS – WELL WORTH THE MONEY

The unrelenting withdrawal of SR steam locomotives during the mid-1960s meant that the variety of classes was rapidly shrinking and consequently the small fleet of USA Class engines suddenly found favour with rail tour organisers. Clearly the capabilities of these locomotives had to be borne in mind but they were ideal for short sections of tours where their low speed would cause no problems. Here a rejuvenated No.30064 waddles down the Guildford to Horsham line near Rudgwick with the 'Midhurst Belle' on 18th October 1964, the scene being considerably enhanced by the brilliant autumn colours. The rail tour organisers did not have to worry about No.30064's lack of speed because this line did not have a Sunday service so the participants had the branch to themselves. *John Beckett*

THE USA CLASS TANKS – WELL WORTH THE MONEY

Some of the most interesting non-passenger workings took place at the opposite end of the SR to the location seen in the previous shot, where trains of perishable produce from Weymouth to Westbury (usually tomatoes from the Channel Islands) were sometimes steam-powered. In this portrait, taken on 18th June 1967, Bulleid 'Light Pacific' No.34102 *Lapford* climbs through Maiden Newton with the 3.00pm Weymouth to Westbury freight working. This unrebuilt Pacific was the last to steam in normal service, being noted on the 6.49am Salisbury to Waterloo passenger and 11.38am van train from Waterloo to Basingstoke on 5th July. It then reportedly ran 'light engine' to Eastleigh where its fire was dropped for the last time. Bridport branch trains used a bay platform with a delightful overall roof, this being clearly visible in the shot. There was a curious mix of both Southern and 'Western' signalling, and other equipment, at Maiden Newton, this being a legacy of its days under SR control from 1950 to 1958. *Charles Whetmath*

This classic, panoramic view of Waterloo station, taken from an adjacent block of flats on 30th June 1967, vividly illustrates how absorbing the railway scene was at that time compared to today's utterly dull uniformity. No wonder train spotters have become an endangered species! The variety of locomotives and rolling stock on view is quite extraordinary, ranging from a green-liveried Brush Type 4 (later Class 47) on the extreme left to a '4-Sub' in blue livery on the far right. Only a handful of blue '4-Sub' units ran with small yellow warning panels and white numerals on the cab front, so this adds considerably to the fascination of this illustration. Also visible is a WR 'Warship' diesel locomotive plus other electric units which appear to include a '4-Cor' and a '2-Hal', both in green, of course. In his excitement the author almost overlooked the steam train in the foreground. This is the 4.40pm boat working to Southampton Docks with Bulleid 'West Country' Class No.34013 *Okehampton* in charge. The formation includes Bulleid coaches in green livery plus a BR Standard brake vehicle in blue/grey colours, which were fashionable at the time. The fifth vehicle, also a BR Standard carriage, appears to be a buffet car in maroon, thus completing this kaleidoscope of railway colours. How absolutely wonderful! *Les Dench*

On the morning of 5th July 1967 the photographer, no doubt conscious of the fact that SR steam traction did not have long to live, undertook a stint of lineside photography at St Denys, just north of Southampton. He was rewarded with quite a reasonable amount of steam activity and the three pictures that follow are a valuable record of steam movements on that morning. The first shot depicts Bulleid 'West Country' Class No.34093 *Saunton,* easing out of an up loop line adjacent to Bevois Park yard with a long-welded rail train in tow, quite a humble job for one of these locomotives. This locomotive's paintwork is in very poor condition, but at least some attempt has been made to smarten up its bedraggled appearance. Strangely, the cabside panels seem to have been painted more recently than the rest of the engine or, perhaps, they just received more enthusiastic cleaning. *Les Dench*

Neatly framed by the girder bridge, the 8.46am Bournemouth to Waterloo (which was due off Southampton at 9.55am) approaches behind No.34013 *Okehampton*, with the crew no doubt taking it easy bearing in mind the train's next stop was at Southampton Airport. This train was a semi-fast working that left Bournemouth fifteen minutes behind 'The Royal Wessex' and was booked to stop at most stations between Bournemouth and Basingstoke, including Lyndhurst Road, Totton and Micheldever. After Basingstoke it called only at Woking, so the locomotive would at last have been given an opportunity to show its capabilities before London was reached. Scheduled arrival time at Waterloo was 12.10pm, more than an hour later than 'The Royal Wessex'. *Les Dench*

The 8.10am Waterloo to Weymouth Quay boat train was, as previously mentioned, one of the most 'reliable' steam-hauled workings and it remained so until the end. On 5th July Bulleid Pacific No.34087 *145 Squadron* powered the train which is seen passing through St Denys with steam to spare. An attempt had obviously been made to improve the locomotive's appearance, but the cleaners could not quite reach the top of the boiler. *Les Dench*

While the attention of most enthusiasts was, understandably, focussed on the high profile passenger workings during the final weeks of SR steam, other workings were also steam hauled, but not really in the limelight. These included an assortment of van, freight and departmental trains throughout the region and one such train is depicted here. The location is near Furzebrook siding, on the Swanage branch, and the train comprises of five wagons of clay from the nearby pits hauled by BR Standard Class 4MT 2-6-4T No.80146, a class not normally seen on freight work. This photograph was taken on 6th July 1967: could it have been the last BR steam train along the branch? Clay production began in the area in the nineteenth century and by 1896 had reached 70,000 tons annually, but declined to 6,000 tons in the 1950s, so this traffic was a real 'money spinner' for the railway for a long period. There were two separate narrow gauge systems serving the clay workings that connected with the branch. All railborne clay traffic ceased in 1972. *Roy Hobbs*

The very distinctive tunnel mouth and extremely deep cutting are excellent clues to this, almost unmistakable, location. It is the southern portal of Bincombe North tunnel, between Dorchester and Weymouth, and the short, three-coach train is the 3.01pm Bournemouth Central to Weymouth with Bulleid 'West Country' Pacific No.34004 *Yeovil* in charge. One of a number of purely local trains between Bournemouth and Weymouth, the 3.01pm called at all stations, apart from Holton Heath; it provided a worthwhile connection out of the 'Bournemouth Belle' which was due into Bournemouth at 2.45pm. This picture was also taken on 6th July 1967. *Roy Hobbs*

During the last months of SR steam many of the locomotives benefited from regular cleaning, at least as much as their blistered paintwork would allow, but the principal beneficiaries of this attention were the Bulleid Pacifics and many of the other engines were untouched. A prime example (grime example?) is BR Standard Class 5MT 4-6-0 No.73020 which is seen here climbing out of Weymouth with a short van train, also on 6th July 1967. This machine had clearly not been cleaned for a long time and was in a terrible state. The roof of Weymouth motive power depot is just visible above the train. *Roy Hobbs*

BR Standard 4-6-0 No.73020 is featured again in this picture of (what appears to be) the 1.30pm Waterloo to Weymouth train threading the New Forest near Sway on 7th July 1967. The photographer recorded that the shot was taken at 4.10pm, so it is almost certainly that train, albeit running a little late. The Lymington branch is clearly visible in the background. No.73020 was outshopped from Derby Works, where the majority of these engines were constructed, in October 1951 and was one of the small number of the SR's allocation of this class active at the end of steam. It was eventually broken-up in January 1968. *Roy Hobbs*

In times gone by Drummond M7 Class 0-4-4Ts were a familiar sight on empty stock and pilot duties at Waterloo, and these machines had to summon up all their reserves of power to drag really heavy formations between there and Clapham Yard, where the stock was serviced. An M7 pulling thirteen coaches may seem a tough assignment, but it really did happen on a daily basis. In the late-1950s redundant WR pannier tank engines were drafted in to Nine Elms shed for some of these workings, but by the mid-1960s Ivatt Class 2MT 2-6-2Ts and BR Standard Class 3MT 2-6-2Ts had largely taken over these chores. This illustration shows No.41298, one of the former class, at Waterloo on 7th July 1967, just a few days before its withdrawal. When SR steam finished Nos.41224/98 and 41312/19/20 were all based on the Southern, and were the very last survivors of their class which thus became extinct on BR when they were withdrawn. *Les Dench*

Much of the steam activity during the final weekend occurred on the Bournemouth to Weymouth section, and in this view the 12.12pm Weymouth to Bournemouth train is depicted arriving at its destination with BR Standard Class 5MT 4-6-0 No.73092 in charge. Despite the fact that the end of steam was imminent, it proved to be a very busy weekend for this particular locomotive which, apparently, later powered the 9.20pm Bournemouth to Eastleigh train. It presumably later worked an overnight train to Weymouth because it appeared on the 2.45pm Weymouth to Westbury tomato train the following day, before working back 'light engine' to Weymouth shed to join the scrap lines. *Charles Whetmath*

Opposite: The last weekend of SR steam saw few workings, except for the melancholy sight of redundant locomotives being moved in groups of two or three to Salisbury, where they congregated prior to being towed away for scrap. One of the last workings into Southampton docks was a two-coach portion off the diesel-hauled 8.35am Waterloo to Weymouth that was detached at Southampton Central and worked forward by BR Standard Class 4MT 2-6-4T No.80152 on 8th July 1967. This formed a through boat train working to the Eastern Docks which is seen here about to cross Canute Road prior to entering the docks area. *Charles Whetmath*

A moment in railway history! An up Ocean Liner Express, the 11.00am from Southampton Eastern Docks to Waterloo, passes over Battledown flyover behind Bulleid Pacific No.34021 *Dartmoor* on 9th July 1967, the last day of steam on the Southern. This was the final steam-worked boat train into Waterloo and one wonders how many of its passengers realised that, purely by chance, they were participating in a very historic event. Earlier in the day BR Standard Class 5MT No.73029 had worked the 9.47am Fratton to Clapham Yard empty coaching stock train, while the honour of powering the *very last* scheduled steam train into Waterloo, and indeed the capital, fell to 'Merchant Navy' Class No.35030 *Elder Dempster Lines*. This machine was used to haul the 2.07pm Weymouth to Waterloo, apparently following a last minute diesel failure, and the plan was that the locomotive would be replaced (presumably by a diesel) at Bournemouth. When the train reached Bournemouth there was considerable indecision as to whether the engine would stay on the train and the locomotive was actually uncoupled at one point. No doubt to the great relief of the assembled multitude of steam fans it was eventually decided that No.35030 would be going through to Waterloo after all. It gave a very competent performance and London was eventually reached ten minutes early. So, at 6.24pm *Elder Dempster Lines* backed out of Waterloo for the last time whistling loudly round the curves out of the terminus. Truly, the end of an era. *Charles Whetmath*

While No.35030 was powering up to London with the last steam-worked express there was considerable steam activity centred on the steeply-graded Weymouth to Westbury cross-country route. A shipload of perishable goods had, apparently, just arrived at Weymouth Quay from the Channel Islands and required immediate onward movement. Three trains were provided, all steam hauled, and represented the largest concentration of steam activity on the last day. Here, BR Standard Class 5MT No.73092 is seen taking the 2.45pm Weymouth to Westbury tomato train through Maiden Newton station, its last major assignment. *John Beckett*

The significance of the chalked slogans on the smokebox door of the locomotive is lost on the author. Perhaps No.73092 had worked a boat train a few days previously but, if so, it does not seem to have been recorded. Maybe it was the handiwork of an enthusiast with a strange sense of humour. The 2.45pm tomato train from Weymouth, the last of three such trains that ran on the final day of SR steam, is seen again approaching Yeovil Pen Mill station, on the short section where the Yeovil Junction to Yeovil Town and Weymouth to Westbury lines ran parallel. Together with the exploits of 'Merchant Navy' Class No.35030 *Elder Dempster Lines*, previously mentioned, and the appearance of BR Standard Class 3MT No.77014 on the 8.50pm Bournemouth to Weymouth van train, this working was also one for the history books, because it was the last known steam freight working on the Southern Region. Furthermore, it was the last steam-worked freight train on the Western Region which, ironically, had declared itself to be a totally 'steam free' zone as long ago as January 1966! *Charles Whetmath*

The other tomato trains to Westbury that ran on 9th July were both hauled by Bulleid Pacifics, No.34095 *Brentor* taking the 10.20am from Weymouth while sister locomotive No.34052 *Lord Dowding,* in quite smart external condition, hauled the 2.20pm *ex*-Weymouth, a very light train compared to No.73092's substantial load. The latter train is also depicted on the four track section near Yeovil. *Charles Whetmath*

All was quiet at Weymouth shed on the morning of 10th July 1967. Steam traction had finally bowed to the inevitable and surrendered to the all-conquering electric and diesel. The new forms of traction may have been cleaner, faster and more efficient but the railways were robbed of much of their unique romance and wonderful, indefinable atmosphere when steam in the south of England disappeared overnight on 9th July 1967. Unbelievably, the job of powering the *very last* main line working fell (as previously mentioned) to BR Standard Class 3MT 2-6-0 No.77014, a class of locomotive that was completely alien to the Southern Region. It is seen here after working into Weymouth with the previous night's 8.50pm parcels train from Bournemouth. The photographer states that the locomotive was still warm after becoming the last steam engine in normal service to arrive in the Dorset town. The arrival of No.77014 on the SR was one of the most unexpected developments during the twilight years of steam traction. It was transferred from Northwich shed, on the LMR, to Guildford and first sighted on the SR on 17th March 1966. This interloper was the only member of its class ever to work in the south of England. It was probably no accident that it had the honour of bringing the curtain down on SR steam and it is more than likely that the working was cleverly organised by enthusiasts employed in the Divisional Manager's Office at Wimbledon. *Colin Caddy*

Photographs: *Michael Chown/Neil Davenport*

Front Cover: Gently does it! Bulleid 'West Country' Pacific No.34037 *Clovelly* eases out of Waterloo station with a Southampton boat extra on 2nd July 1967. This was the day that BR, rather strangely, chose to operate two commemorative specials to mark the end of Southern steam and participants must have been annoyed to find that they could have travelled behind No.34025 *Whimple* on the 9.33am excursion to Bournemouth at a fraction of the fare being charged for the special trains. At least the engine crews on the specials entered into the spirit of the occasion (such as it was!) and the Waterloo to Weymouth train reached speeds of 88mph on the down journey whilst a very creditable 90mph was attained on the return run. Motive power on the Weymouth train was 'Merchant Navy' Pacific No.35008 *Orient Line,* while a special to Bournemouth and back was hauled by No.35028 *Clan Line.* Both locomotives were turned out in exemplary condition. *Michael Chown*

Back cover: Maunsell 'Mogul' Nos. 31405 and 31858 are seen on ballast duty at Fleet on a very icy 14th November 1966. *Charles Whetmath*

Title page: Dereliction and decay at Nine Elms shed during the last days of steam. *Alan Chandler*